FOR ORGANS, PIANOS & ELECTRONIC KEYBOARDS

E-Z PLAY® TODAY

117

TONY BENNETT
ALL TIME GREATEST HITS

T0068382

Photos by Don Hunstein, courtesy of Sony/Columbia Records.

ISBN 978-1-5400-4606-2

For all works contained herein:
Unauthorized copying, arranging, adapting, recording, Internet posting, public performance,
or other distribution of the music in this publication is an infringement of copyright.
Infringers are liable under the law.

E-Z Play ® TODAY Music Notation © 1975 HAL LEONARD LLC
E-Z PLAY and EASY ELECTRONIC KEYBOARD MUSIC are registered trademarks of HAL LEONARD LLC.

Visit Hal Leonard Online at
www.halleonard.com

Contact us:
Hal Leonard
7777 West Bluemound Road
Milwaukee, WI 53213
Email: info@halleonard.com

In Europe, contact:
Hal Leonard Europe Limited
42 Wigmore Street
Marylebone, London, W1U 2RN
Email: info@halleonardeurope.com

In Australia, contact:
Hal Leonard Australia Pty. Ltd.
4 Lentara Court
Cheltenham, Victoria, 3192 Australia
Email: info@halleonard.com.au

Registration Guide

• Match the Registration number on the song to the corresponding numbered category below. Select and activate an instrumental sound available on your instrument.

• Choose an automatic rhythm appropriate to the mood and style of the song. (Consult your Owner's Guide for proper operation of automatic rhythm features.)

• Adjust the tempo and volume controls to comfortable settings.

Registration

1	Mellow	Flutes, Clarinet, Oboe, Flugel Horn, Trombone, French Horn, Organ Flutes
2	Ensemble	Brass Section, Sax Section, Wind Ensemble, Full Organ, Theater Organ
3	Strings	Violin, Viola, Cello, Fiddle, String Ensemble, Pizzicato, Organ Strings
4	Guitars	Acoustic/Electric Guitars, Banjo, Mandolin, Dulcimer, Ukulele, Hawaiian Guitar
5	Mallets	Vibraphone, Marimba, Xylophone, Steel Drums, Bells, Celesta, Chimes
6	Liturgical	Pipe Organ, Hand Bells, Vocal Ensemble, Choir, Organ Flutes
7	Bright	Saxophones, Trumpet, Mute Trumpet, Synth Leads, Jazz/Gospel Organs
8	Piano	Piano, Electric Piano, Honky Tonk Piano, Harpsichord, Clavi
9	Novelty	Melodic Percussion, Wah Trumpet, Synth, Whistle, Kazoo, Perc. Organ
10	Bellows	Accordion, French Accordion, Mussette, Harmonica, Pump Organ, Bagpipes

CONTENTS

4   The Best Is Yet To Come

6   Cheek To Cheek

8   Don't Get Around Much Anymore

14 Everybody's Talkin' (Echoes)

16 Fly Me To The Moon (In Other Words)

18 For Once in My Life

11 The Good Life

20 I Left My Heart In San Francisco

22 I Wanna Be Around

24 It Had To Be You

30 Just In Time

32 Night And Day

34 One For My Baby (And One More For The Road)

36 Put On A Happy Face

38 Rags To Riches

27 A Rainy Day

40 Sing, You Sinners

42 Smile

44 Something

46 Steppin' Out With My Baby

49 Stranger In Paradise

58 Take The "A" Train

52 Where Do I Begin (Love Theme)

56 Who Can I Turn To (When Nobody Needs Me)

The Best Is Yet to Come

Registration 7
Rhythm: Swing

Music by Cy Coleman
Lyrics by Carolyn Leigh

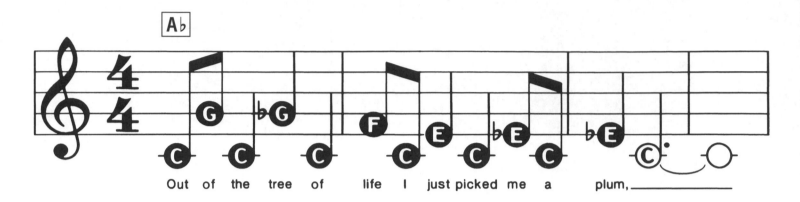

Out of the tree of life I just picked me a plum,_____

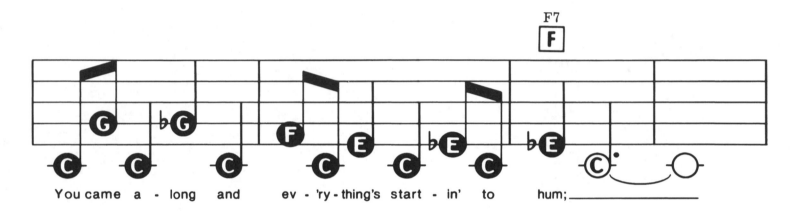

You came a - long and ev - 'ry-thing's start - in' to hum;_____

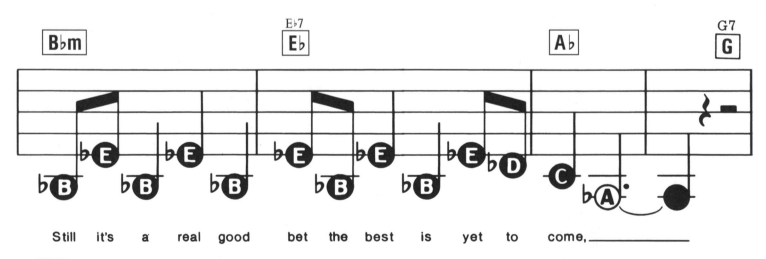

Still it's a real good bet the best is yet to come,_____

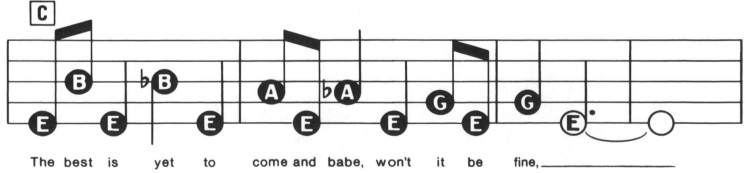

The best is yet to come and babe, won't it be fine,_____

Copyright © 1959, 1961 Notable Music Company, Inc. and EMI Carwin Music Inc.
Copyright Renewed
All Rights for Notable Music Company, Inc. Administered by Words & Music
Exclusive Print Rights for EMI Carwin Music Inc. Administered by Alfred Music
All Rights Reserved   Used by Permission

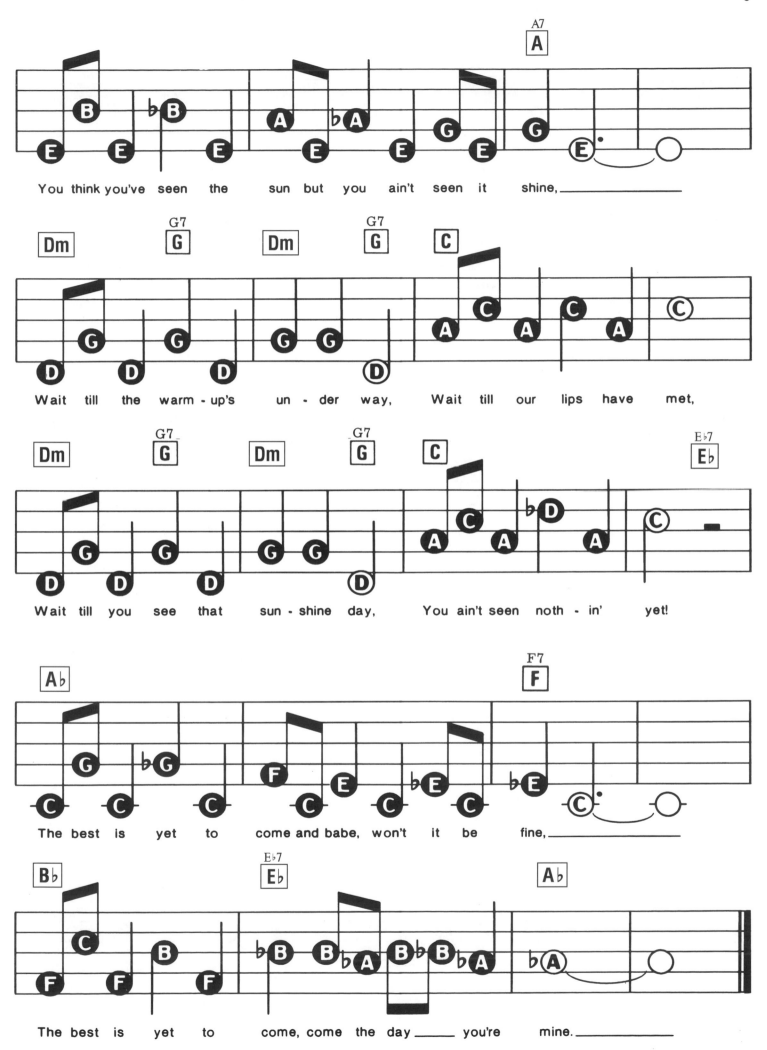

Cheek to Cheek
from the RKO Radio Motion Picture TOP HAT

Registration 1
Rhythm: Fox Trot or Swing

Words and Music by
Irving Berlin

© Copyright 1935 by Irving Berlin
Copyright Renewed
International Copyright Secured   All Rights Reserved

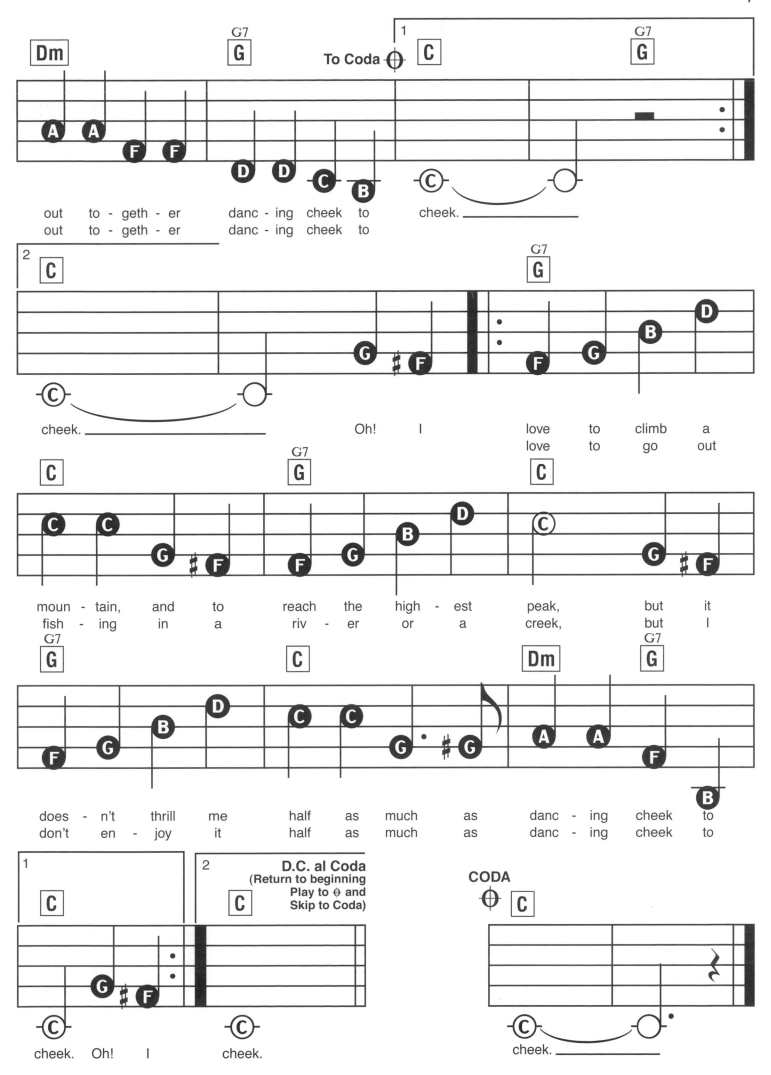

Don't Get Around Much Anymore

Registration 7
Rhythm: Swing

Words and Music by Duke Ellington
and Bob Russell

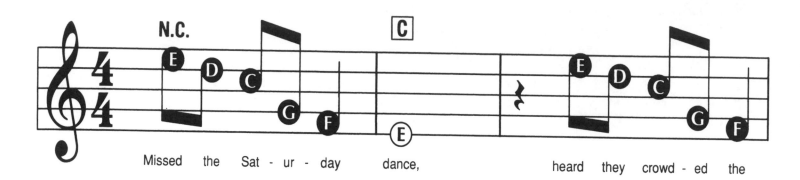

Missed the Sat - ur - day dance, heard they crowd - ed the

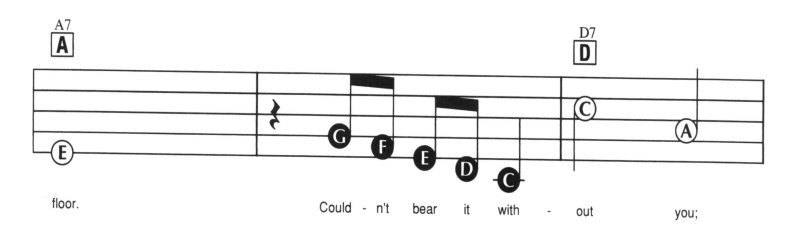

floor. Could - n't bear it with - out you;

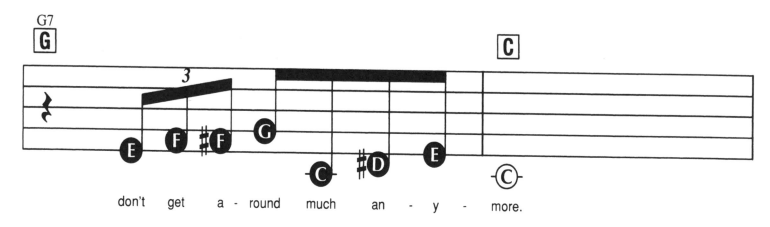

don't get a - round much an - y - more.

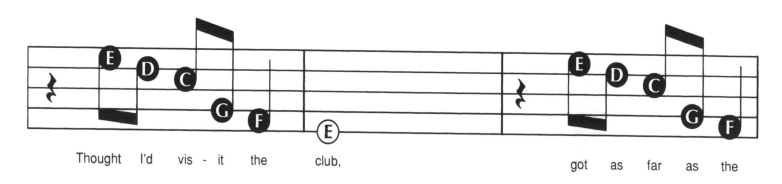

Thought I'd vis - it the club, got as far as the

Copyright © 1942, 1943 Sony/ATV Music Publishing LLC and Harrison Music Corp
Copyright Renewed
All Rights on behalf of Sony/ATV Music Publishing LLC Administered by Sony/ATV Music Publishing LLC, 424 Church Street, Suite 1200, Nashville, TN 37219
All Rights on behalf of Harrison Music Corp. Administered by Music Sales Corporation
International Copyright Secured   All Rights Reserved

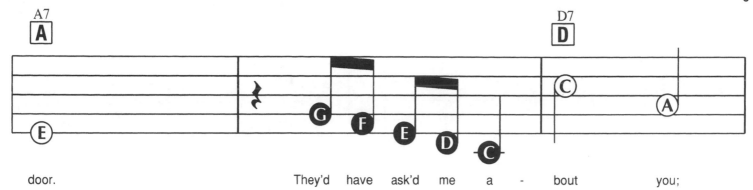

door.   They'd have ask'd me a - bout you;

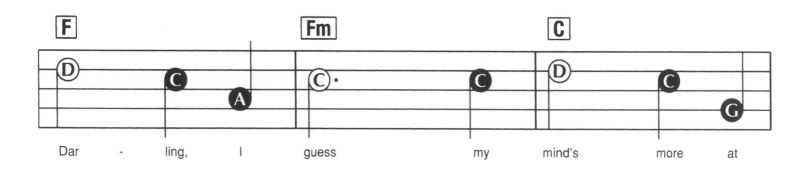

don't get a - round much an - y - more.

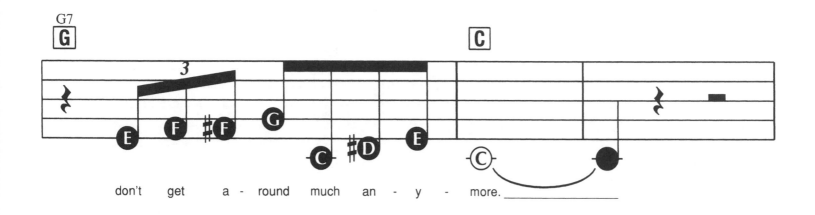

Dar - ling, I guess my mind's more at

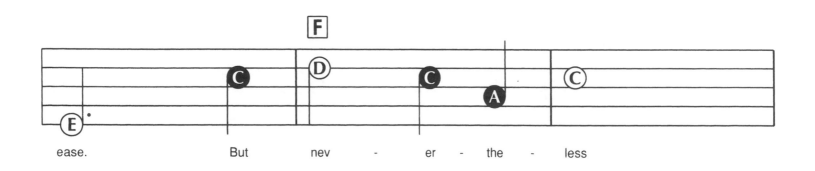

ease.   But nev - er - the - less

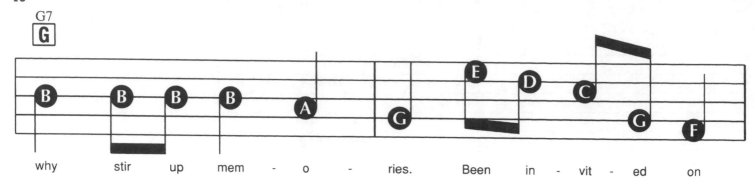

why stir up mem - o - ries. Been in - vit - ed on

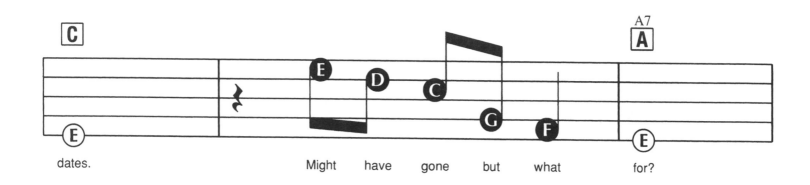

dates. Might have gone but what for?

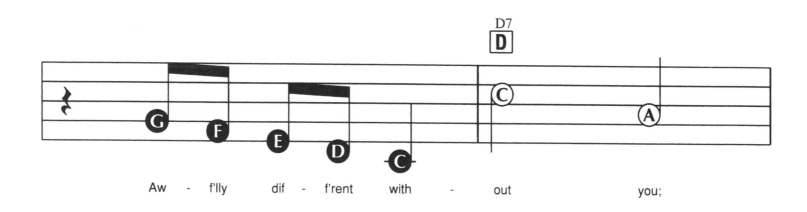

Aw - f'lly dif - f'rent with - out you;

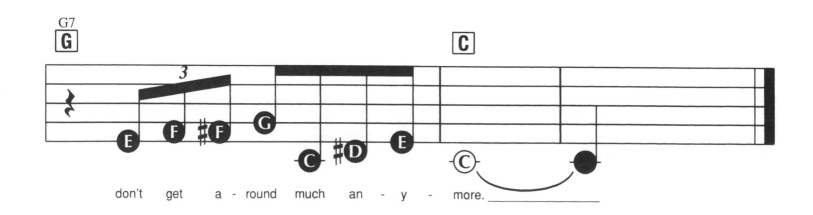

don't get a - round much an - y - more.

The Good Life

Registration 8
Rhythm: Ballad or Fox Trot

Words by Jack Reardon
Music by Sacha Distel

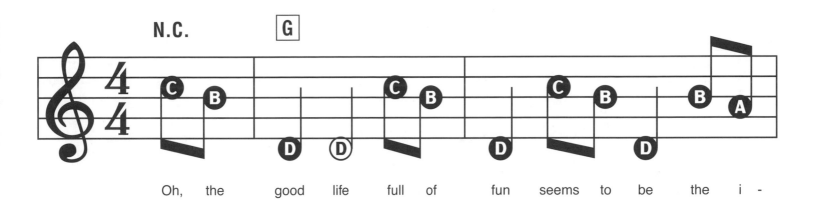

Oh, the good life full of fun seems to be the i-

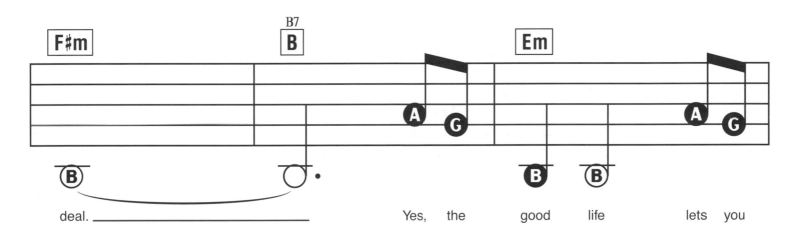

deal. _____ Yes, the good life lets you

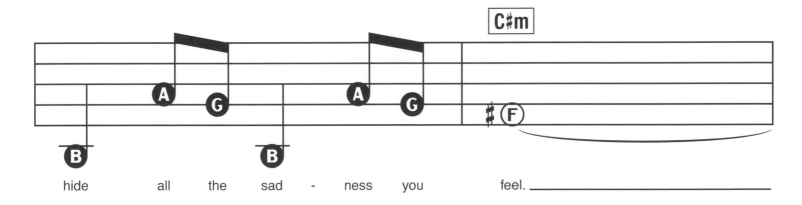

hide all the sad - ness you feel. _____

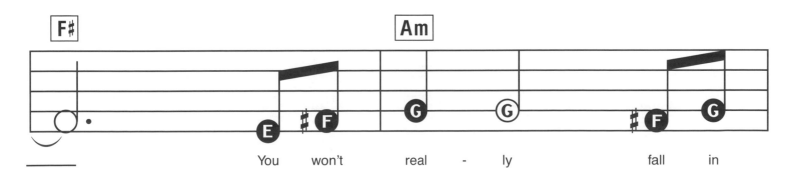

_____ You won't real - ly fall in

© 1962 (Renewed) WB MUSIC CORP. and DIFFUSION MUSICALES FRANCAISE
All Rights for DIFFUSION MUSICALES FRANCAISE in the U.S. and Canada Administered by INTERSONG U.S.A., INC.
All Rights Reserved   Used by Permission

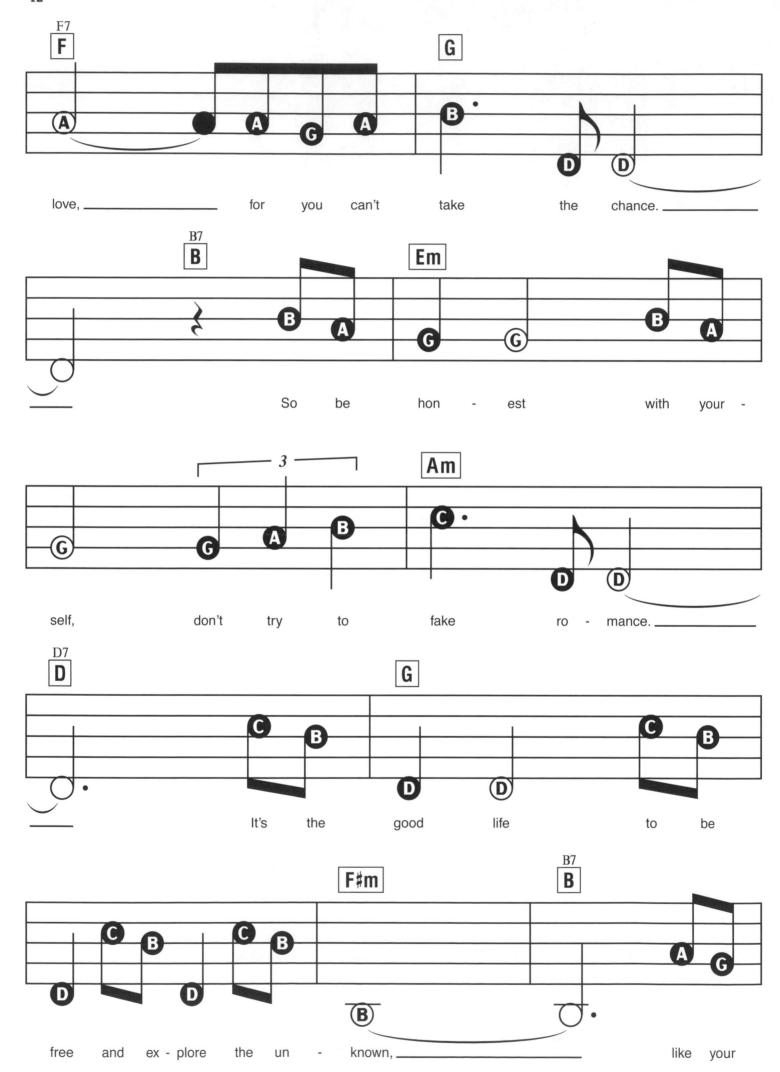

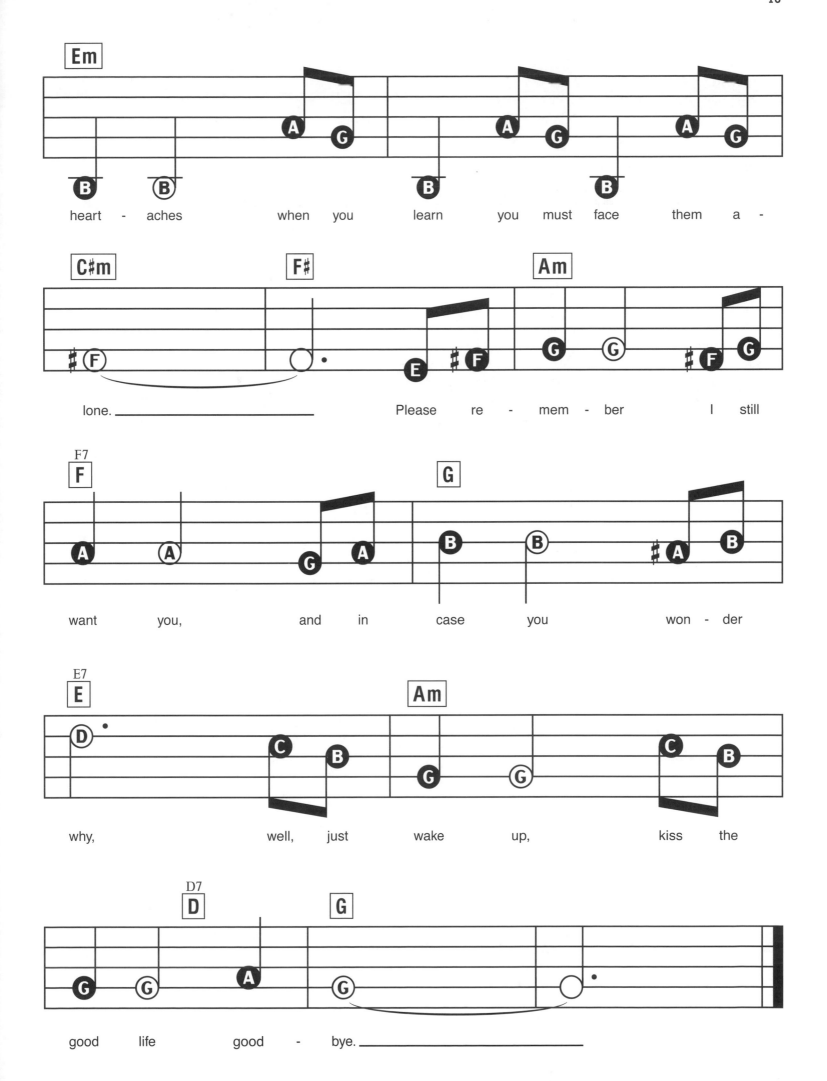

Everybody's Talkin'

(Echoes)

Registration 6
Rhythm: Rock

Words and Music by
Fred Neil

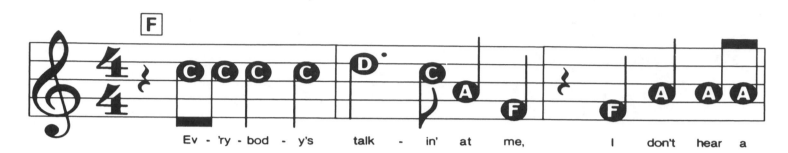

Ev - 'ry - bod - y's talk - in' at me, I don't hear a

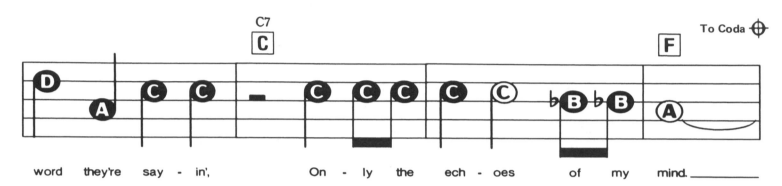

word they're say - in', On - ly the ech - oes of my mind. _____

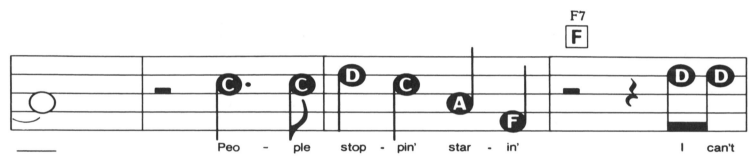

Peo - ple stop - pin' star - in' I can't

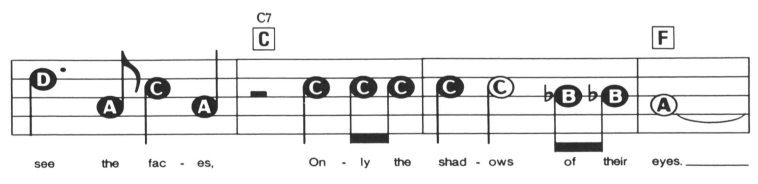

see the fac - es, On - ly the shad - ows of their eyes. _____

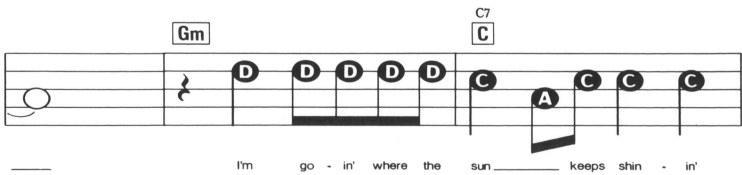

_____ I'm go - in' where the sun keeps shin - in'

Copyright © 1967 (Renewed) Third Palm Music (BMI)
Worldwide Rights owned by Arc Music, Inc. (Administered by BMG Rights Management (US) LLC)
All Rights Reserved   Used by Permission

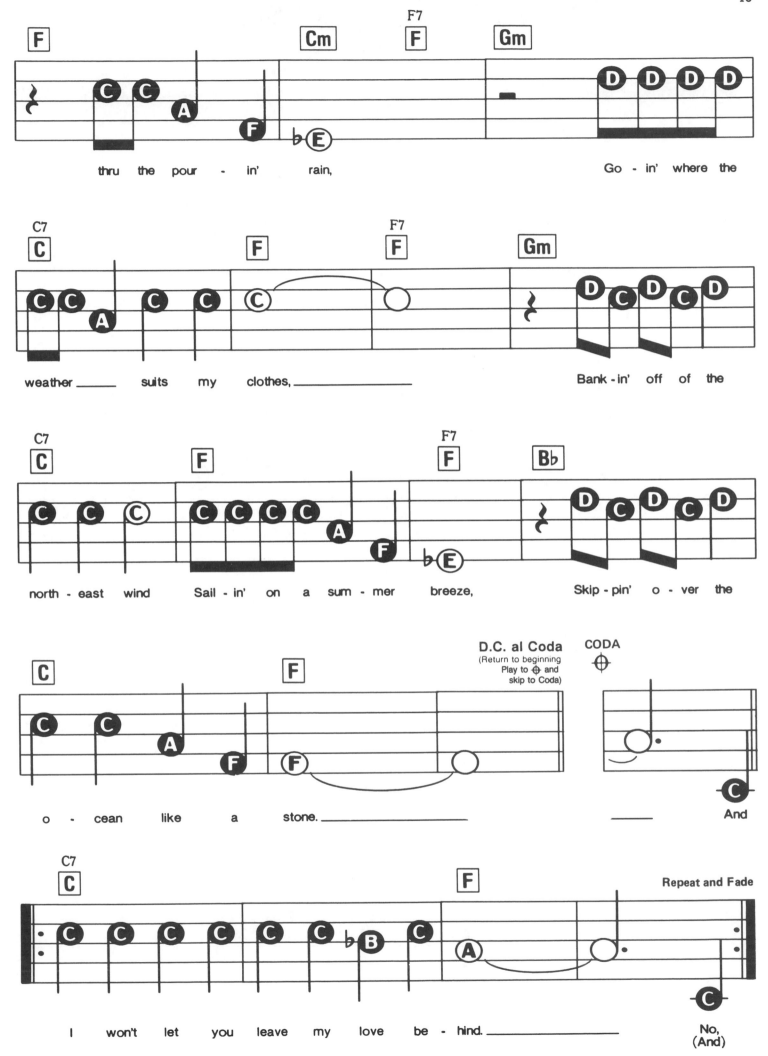

Fly Me to the Moon
(In Other Words)

Registration 2
Rhythm: Waltz or Jazz Waltz

Words and Music by
Bart Howard

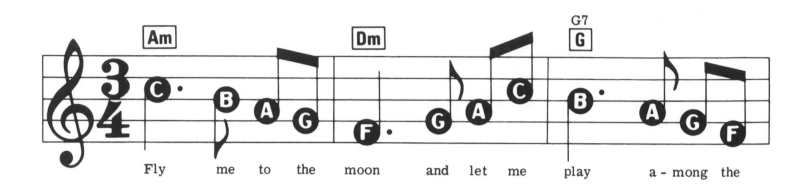

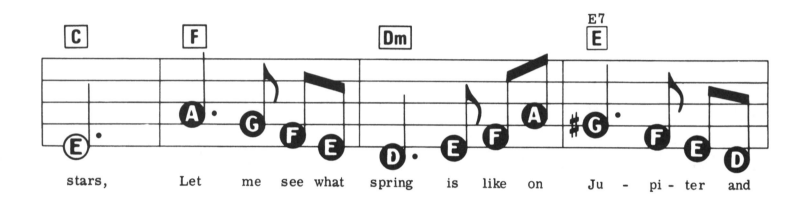

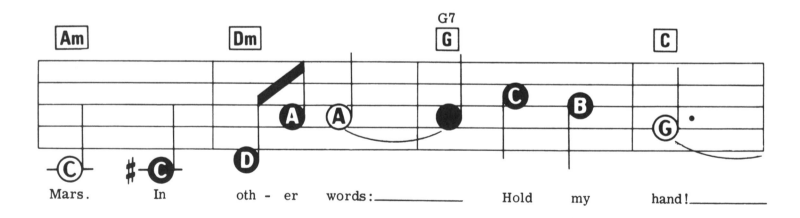

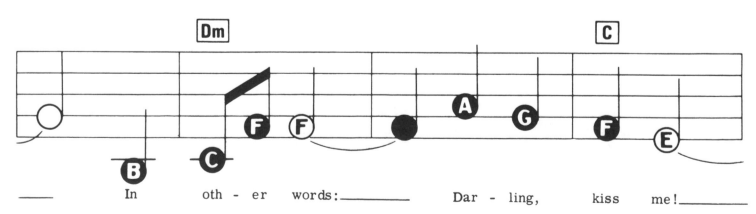

TRO - © Copyright 1954 (Renewed) Palm Valley Music, L.L.C., New York, NY
International Copyright Secured
All Rights Reserved Including Public Performance For Profit
Used by Permission

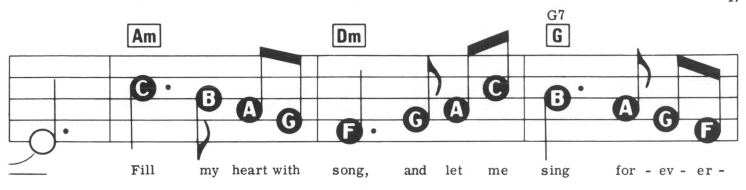

Fill my heart with song, and let me sing for - ev - er -

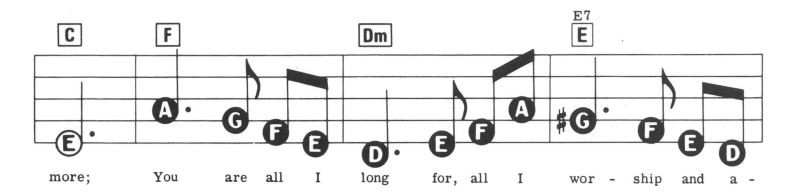

more; You are all I long for, all I wor - ship and a -

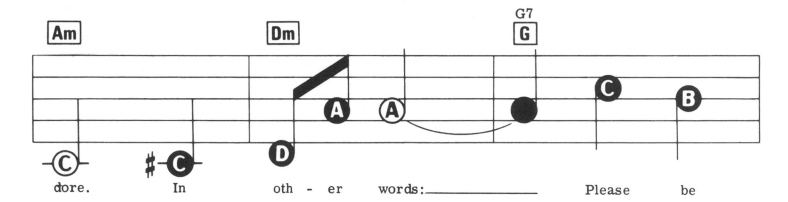

dore. In oth - er words:_____ Please be

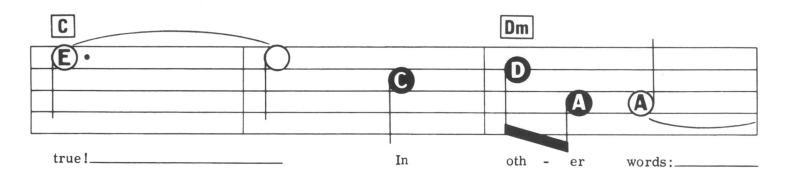

true!_____ In oth - er words:_____

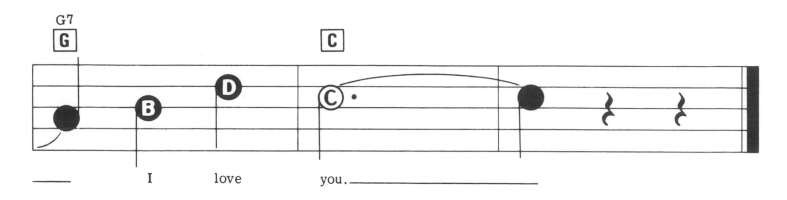

_____ I love you._____

For Once in My Life

Registration 8
Rhythm: Rock or Pops

Words by Ronald Miller
Music by Orlando Murden

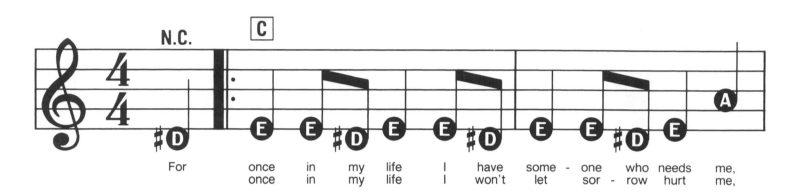

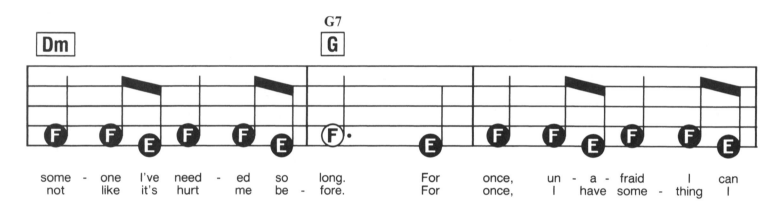

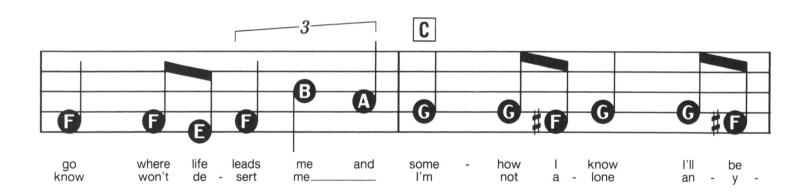

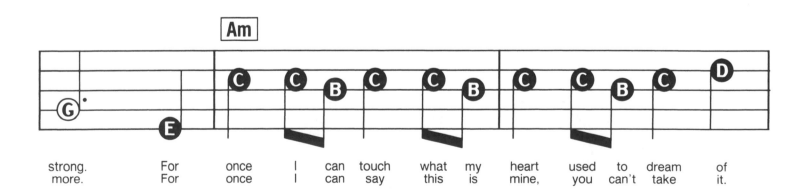

© 1965 Jobete Music Co., Inc. and Stone Diamond Music Corp.
All Rights Administered by Sony/ATV Music Publishing LLC, 424 Church Street, Suite 1200, Nashville, TN 37219
International Copyright Secured   All Rights Reserved

19

I Left My Heart in San Francisco

Registration 9
Rhythm: Fox Trot

Words by Douglass Cross
Music by George Cory

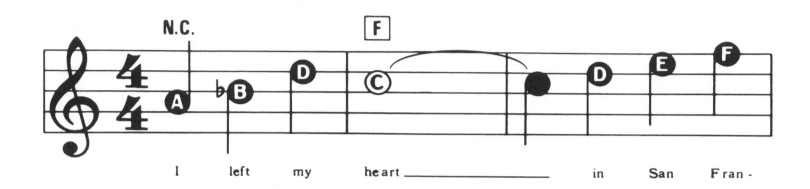

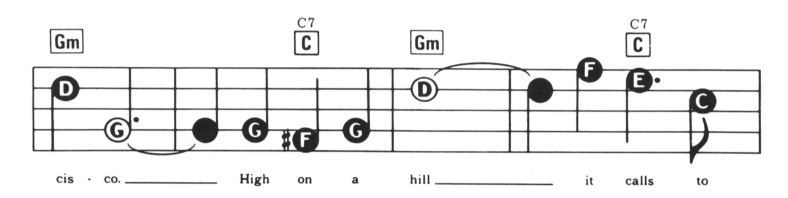

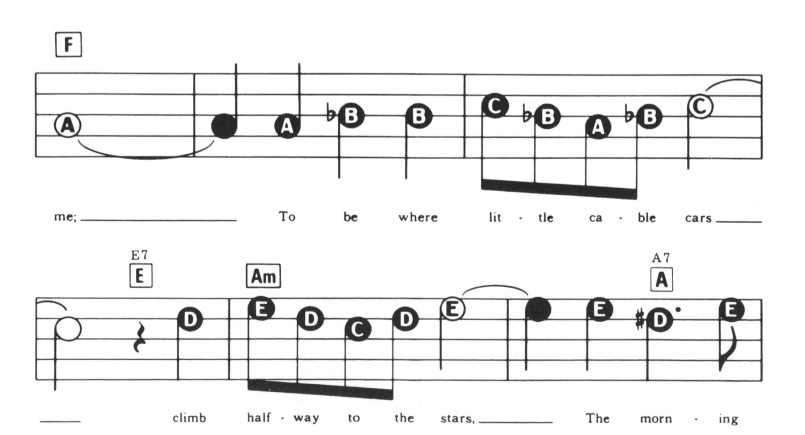

Copyright © 1954 Colgems-EMI Music Inc.
Copyright Renewed
All Rights Administered by Sony/ATV Music Publishing LLC, 424 Church Street, Suite 1200, Nashville, TN
International Copyright Secured   All Rights Reserved

21

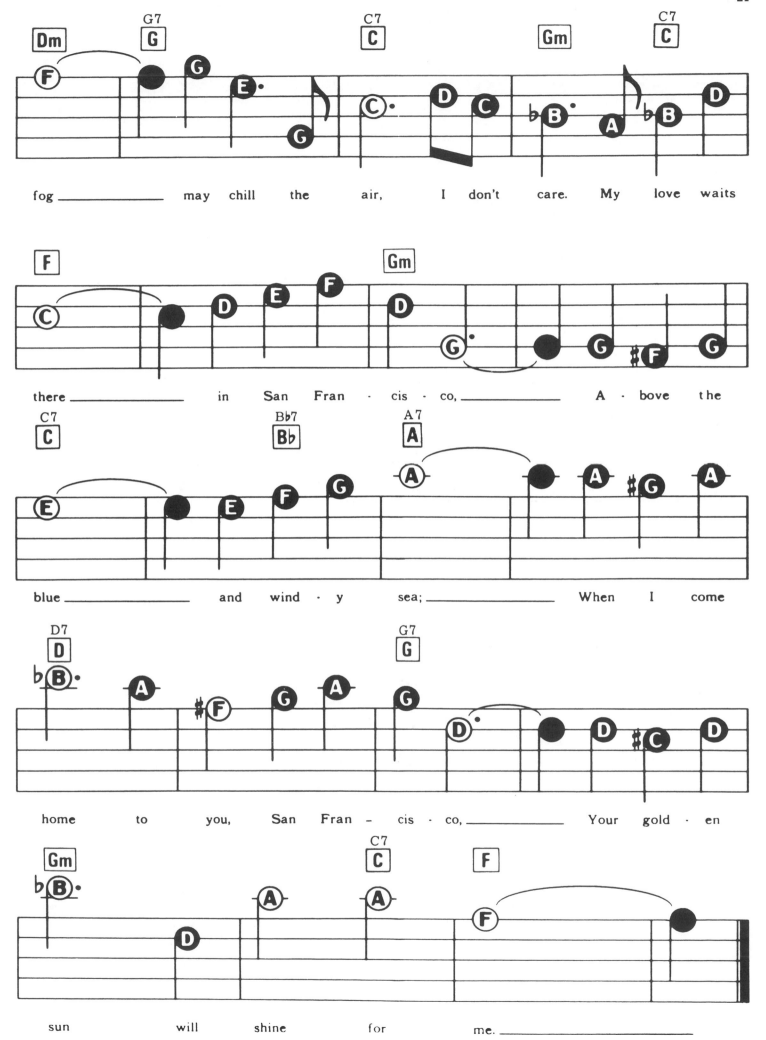

I Wanna Be Around

Registration 4
Rhythm: Swing or Jazz

Words by Johnny Mercer
Music by Sadie Vimmerstedt

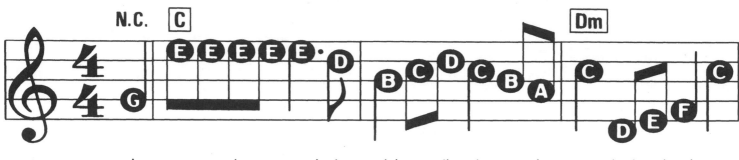

I wan-na be a-round to pick up the piec-es, when some-bod-y breaks your

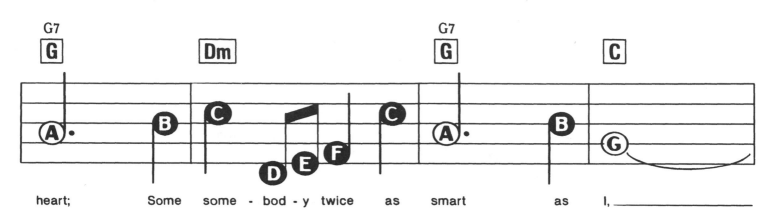

heart; Some some-bod-y twice as smart as I, _____

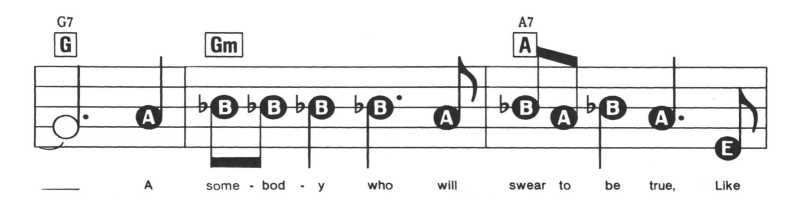

_____ A some-bod-y who will swear to be true, Like

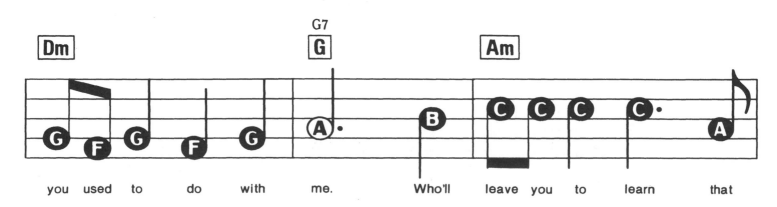

you used to do with me. Who'll leave you to learn that

© 1959 (Renewed) WB MUSIC CORP.
All Rights Reserved Used by Permission

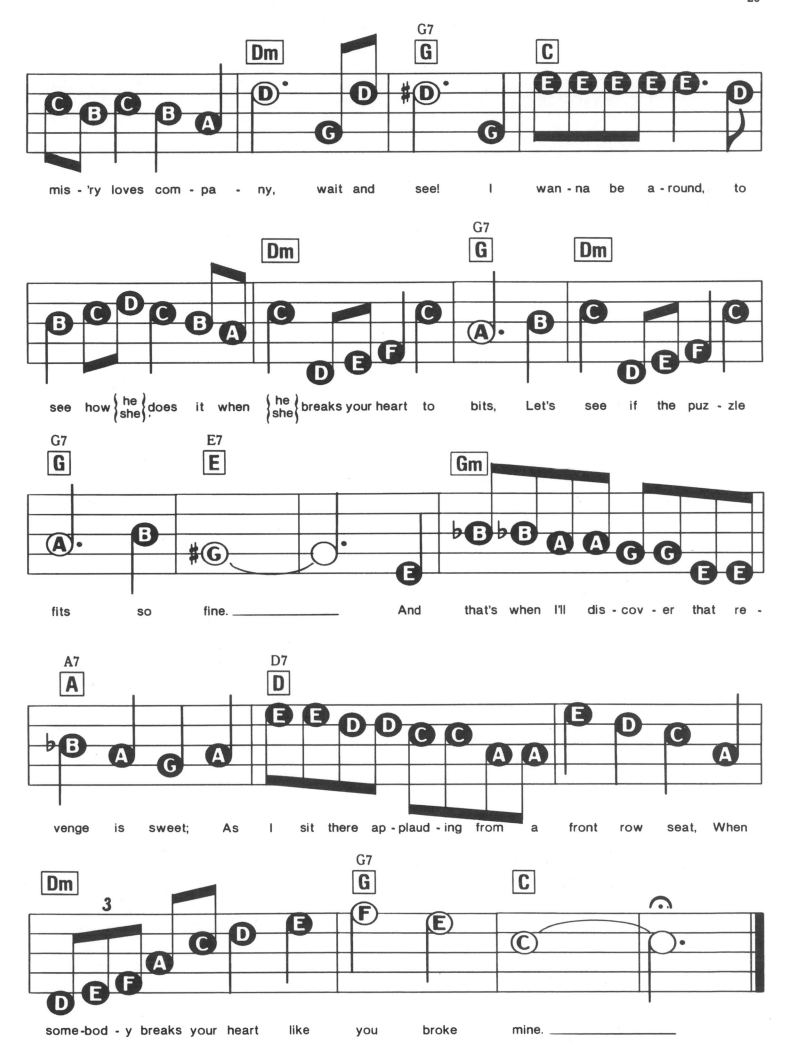

It Had to Be You

Registration 9
Rhythm: Swing

Words by Gus Kahn
Music by Isham Jones

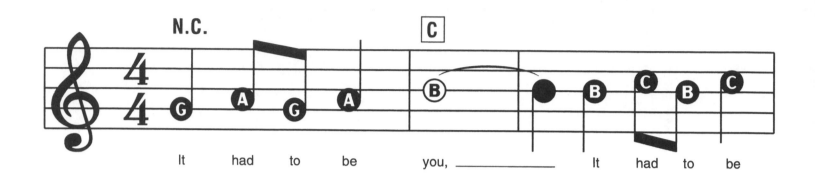

It had to be you, _____ It had to be

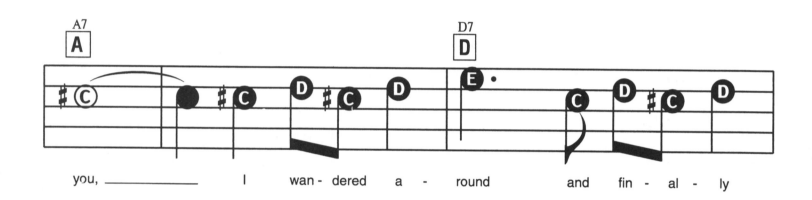

you, _____ I wan - dered a - round and fin - al - ly

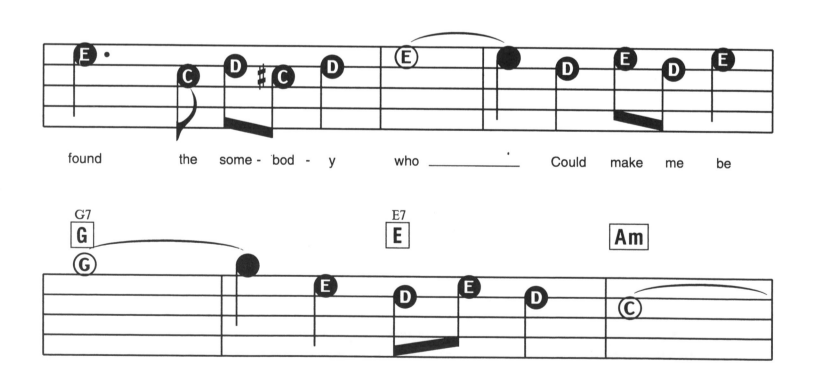

found the some - bod - y who _____ Could make me be

true, _____ could make me be blue _____

© 1924 (Renewed) GILBERT KEYES MUSIC and THE BANTAM MUSIC PUBLISHING CO.
All Rights Administered by WB MUSIC CORP.
All Rights Reserved   Used by Permission

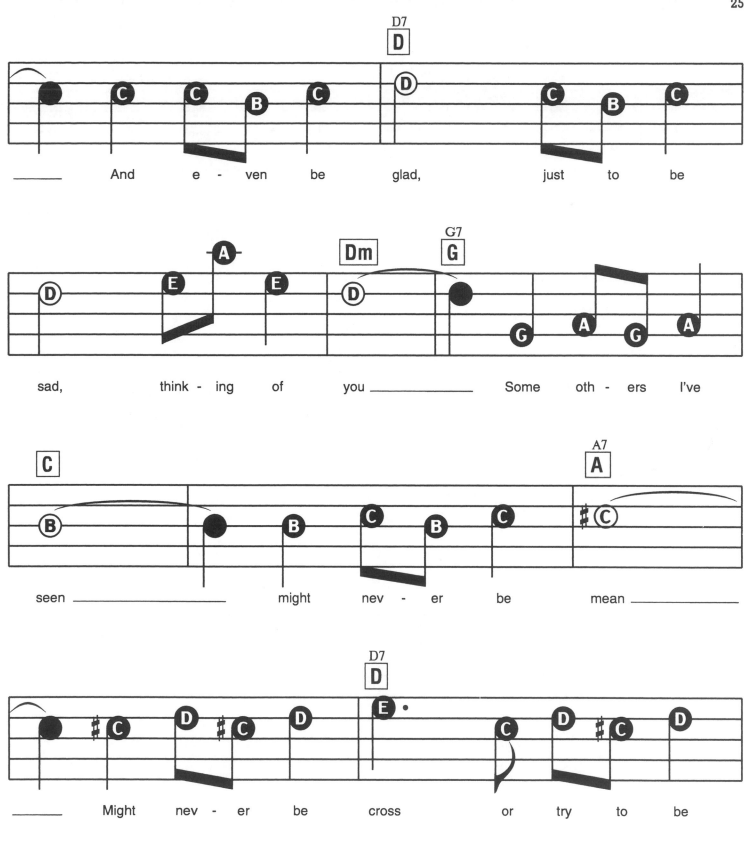

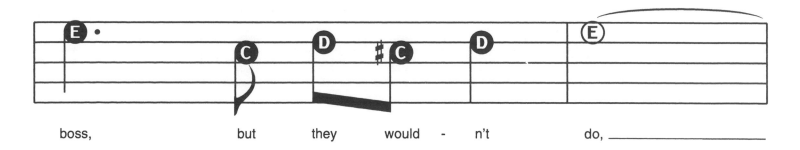

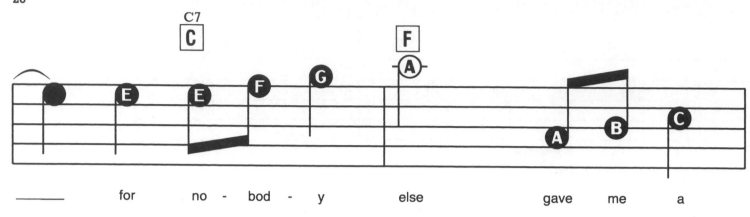

for no - bod - y else gave me a

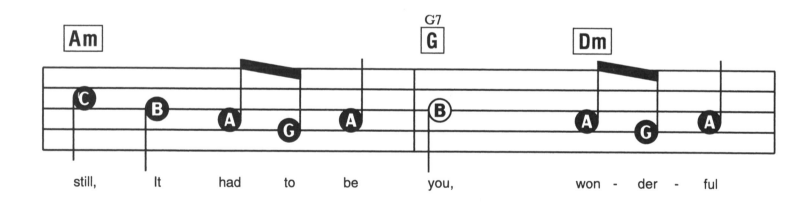

thrill, with all your faults I love you

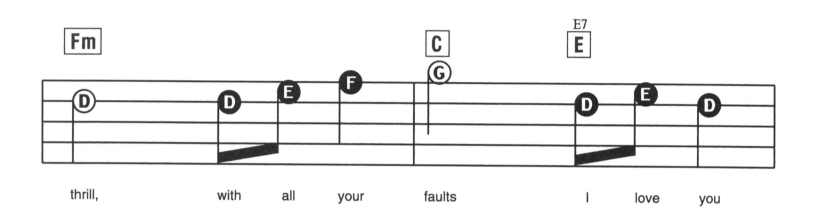

still, It had to be you, won - der - ful

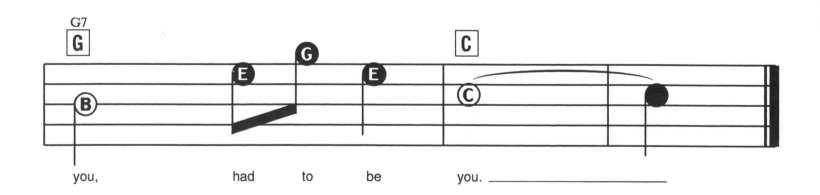

you, had to be you. _____

A Rainy Day

Registration 2
Rhythm: Fox Trot or Swing

Words by Howard Dietz
Music by Arthur Schwartz

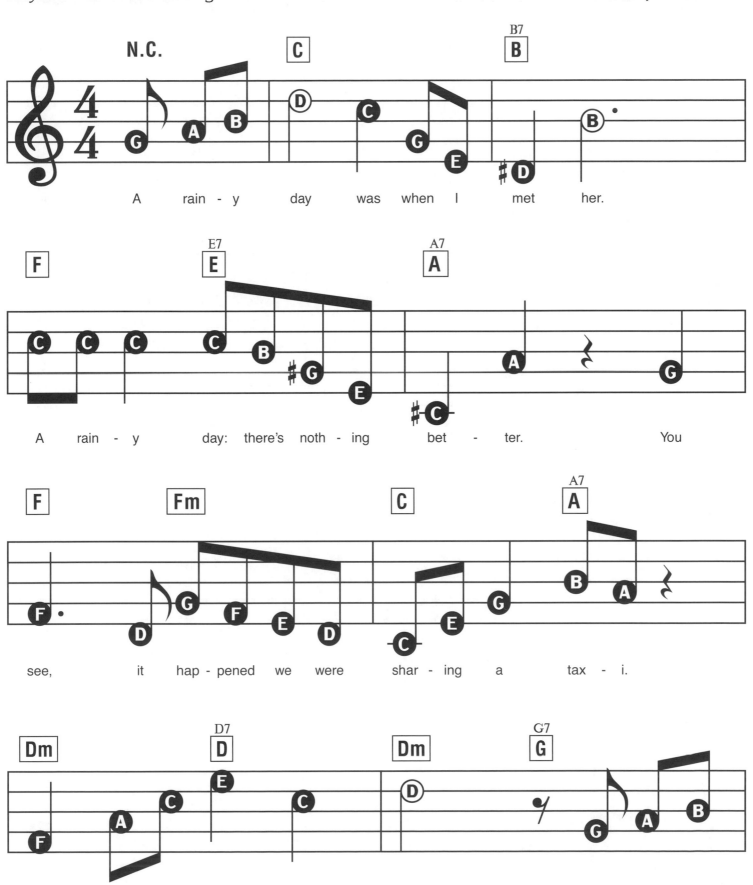

© 1932 (Renewed) WB MUSIC CORP. and ARTHUR SCHWARTZ MUSIC LTD.
All Rights Reserved   Used by Permission

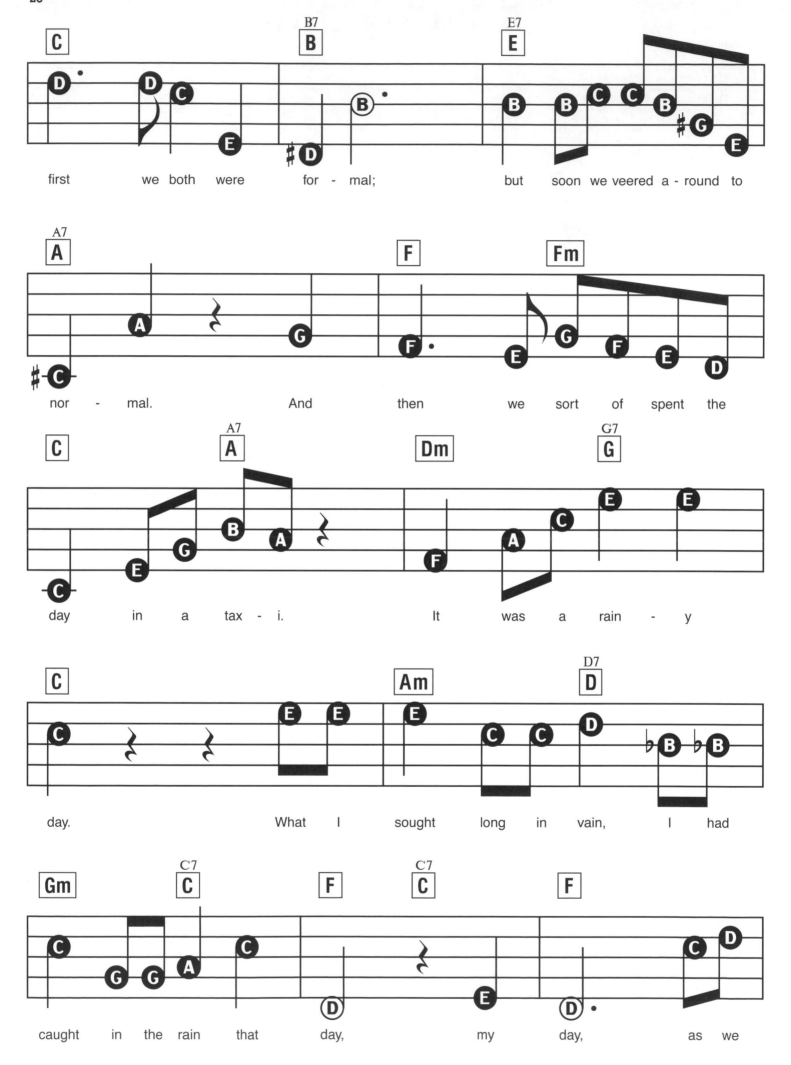

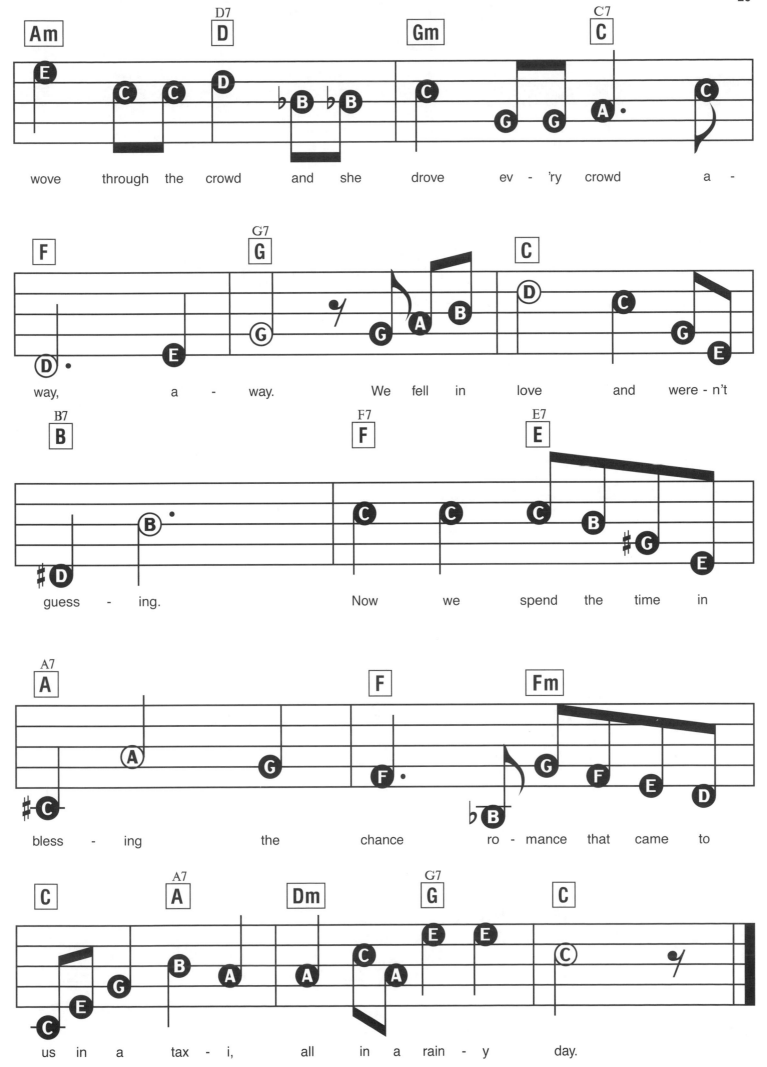

Just in Time
from BELLS ARE RINGING

Registration 2
Rhythm: Fox Trot or Swing

Words by Betty Comden
and Adolph Green
Music by Jule Styne

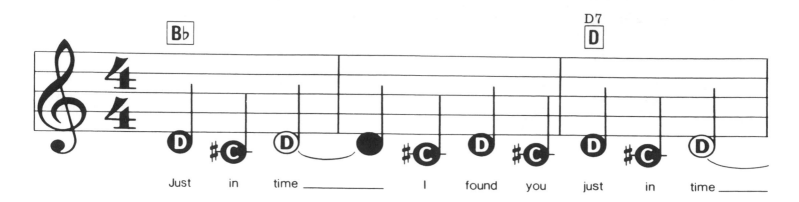

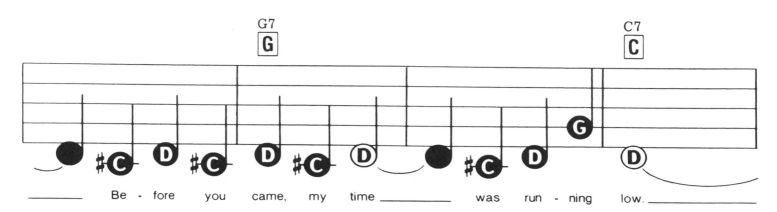

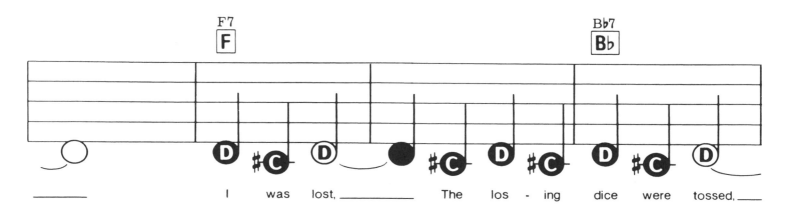

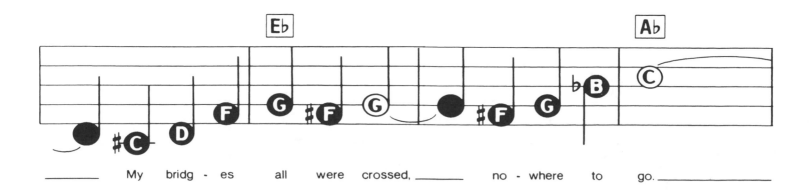

© 1956 (Renewed) BETTY COMDEN, ADOLPH GREEN and JULE STYNE
STRATFORD MUSIC CORP., Owner of Publication and Allied Rights throughout the World
All Rights Administered by CHAPPELL & CO., INC.
All Rights Reserved   Used by Permission

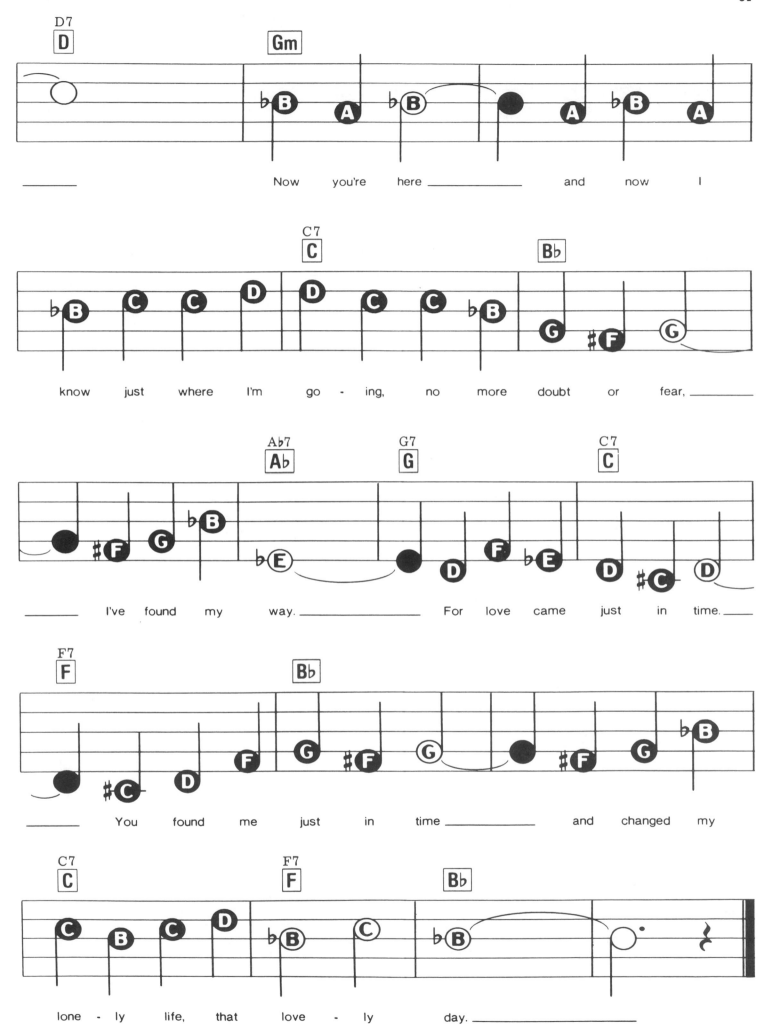

Night and Day

Registration 7
Rhythm: Fox Trot or Swing

Words and Music by
Cole Porter

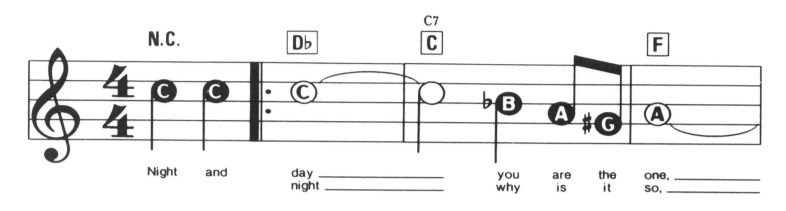

Night and day _____ you are the one, _____
night _____ why is it so, _____

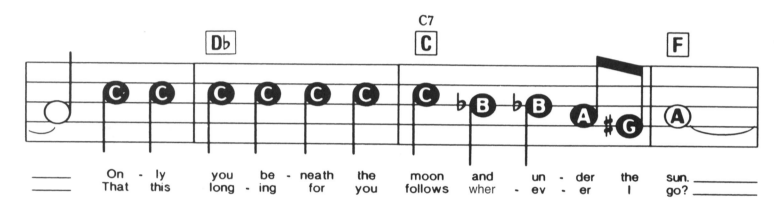

_____ On - ly you be - neath the moon and un - der the sun. _____
_____ That this long - ing for you follows wher - ev - er I go? _____

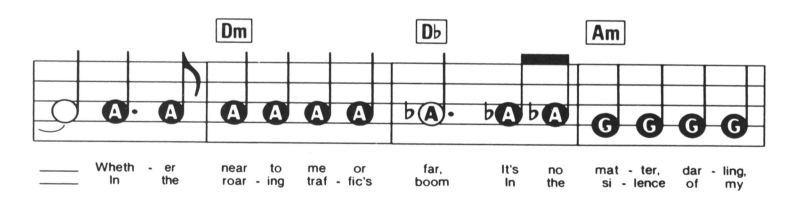

_____ Wheth - er near to me or far, It's no mat - ter, dar - ling,
_____ In the roar - ing traf - fic's boom In the si - lence of my

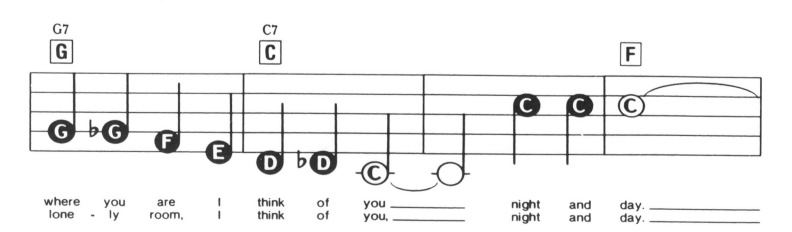

where you are I think of you _____ night and day.
lone - ly room, I think of you, _____ night and day.

© 1934 (Renewed) WB MUSIC CORP.
All Rights Reserved   Used by Permission

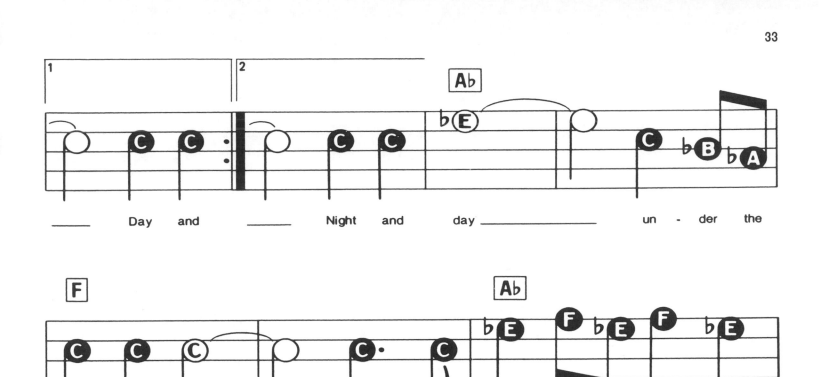

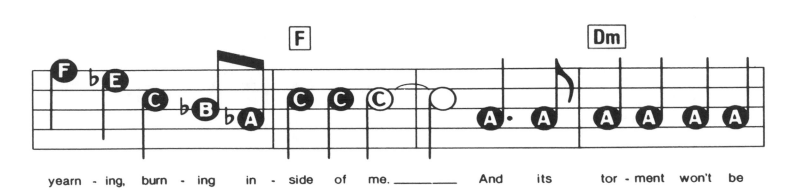

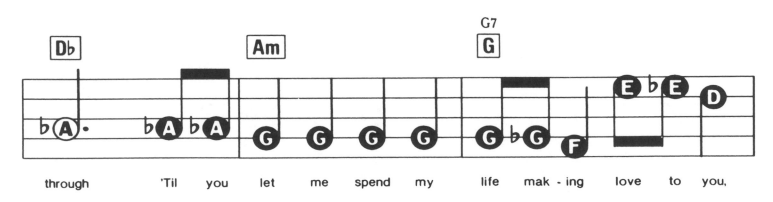

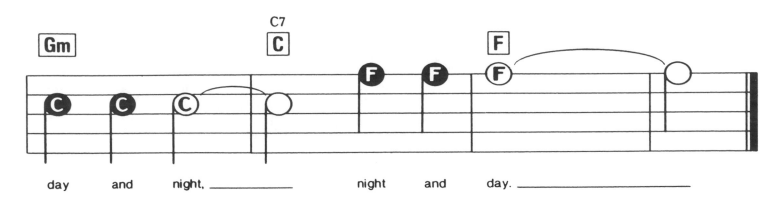

One for My Baby
(And One More for the Road)

Registration 2
Rhythm: Swing

Lyric by Johnny Mercer
Music by Harold Arlen

© 1943 (Renewed) HARWIN MUSIC CO.
All Rights Reserved

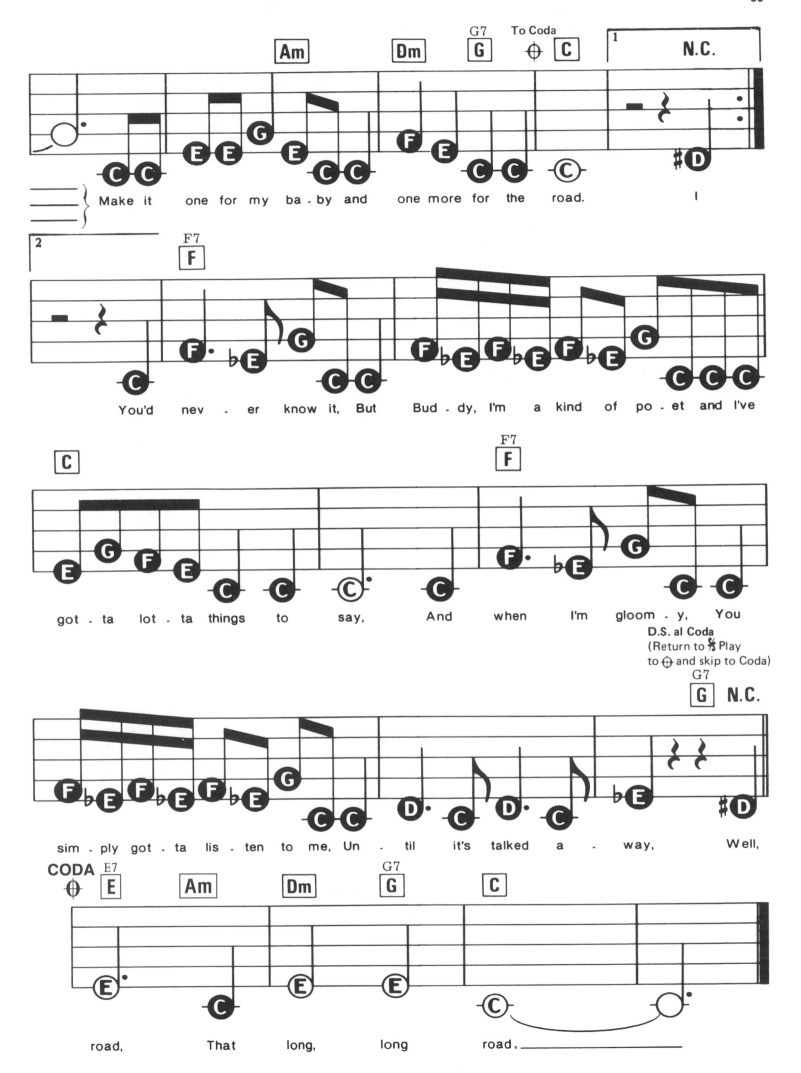

Put On a Happy Face
from BYE BYE BIRDIE

Registration 5
Rhythm: Swing

Lyric by Lee Adams
Music by Charles Strouse

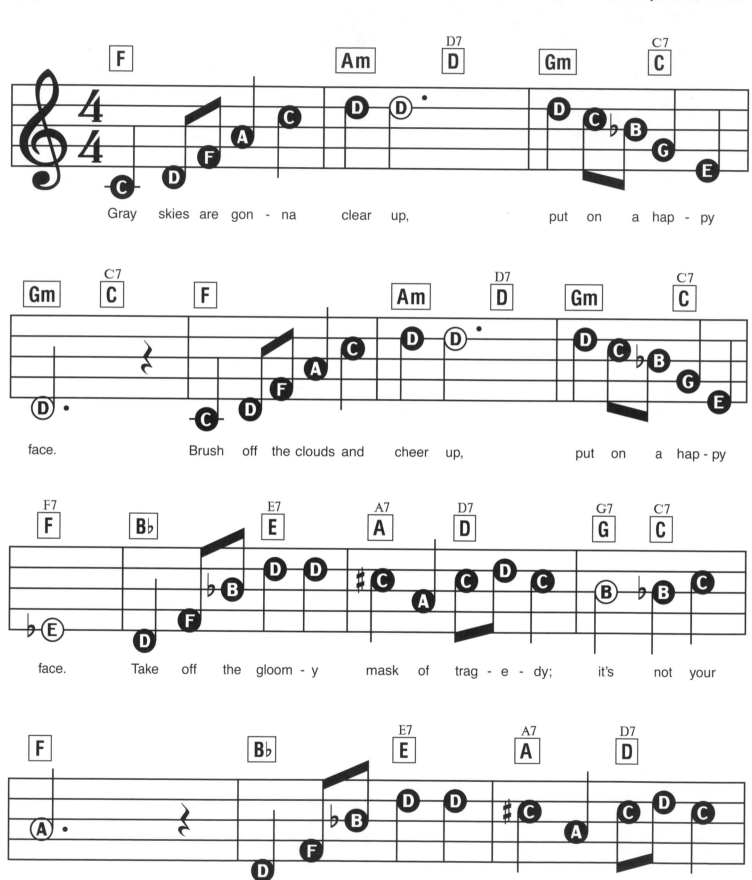

© 1960 (Renewed) STRADA MUSIC
All Rights Administered by WB MUSIC CORP.
All Rights Reserved   Used by Permission

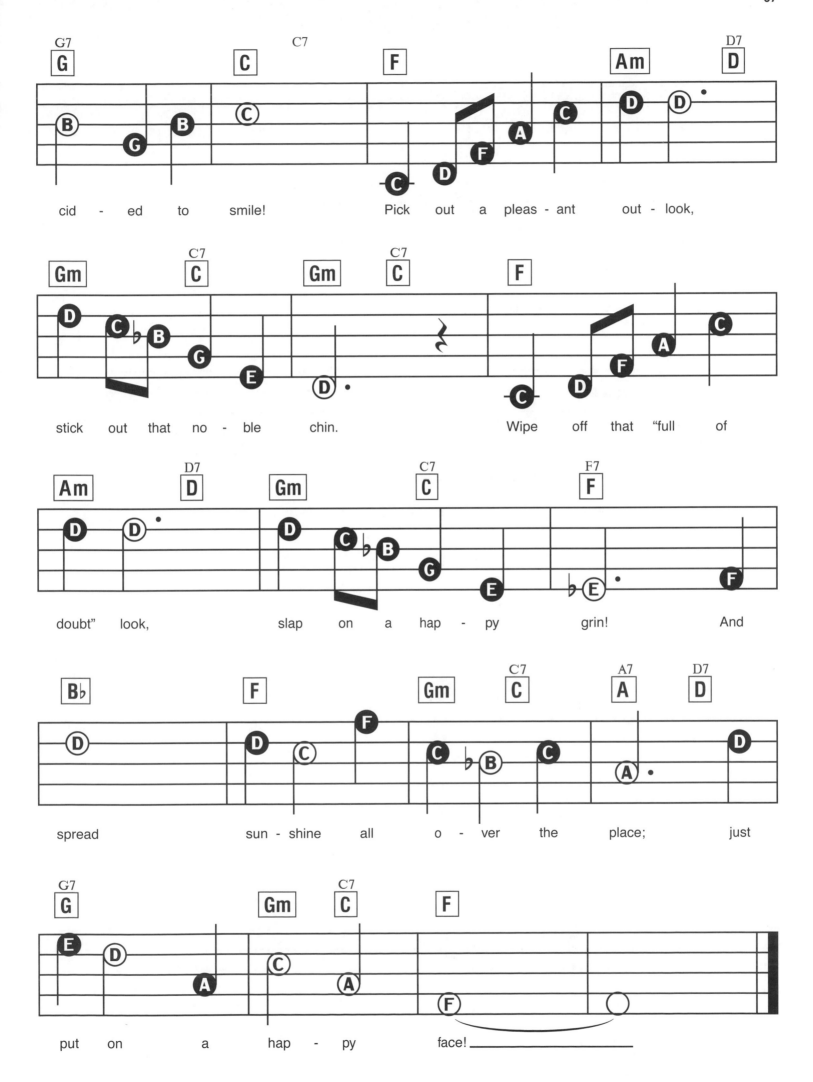

Rags to Riches

Registration 7
Rhythm: Swing or Ballad

Words and Music by Richard Adler
and Jerry Ross

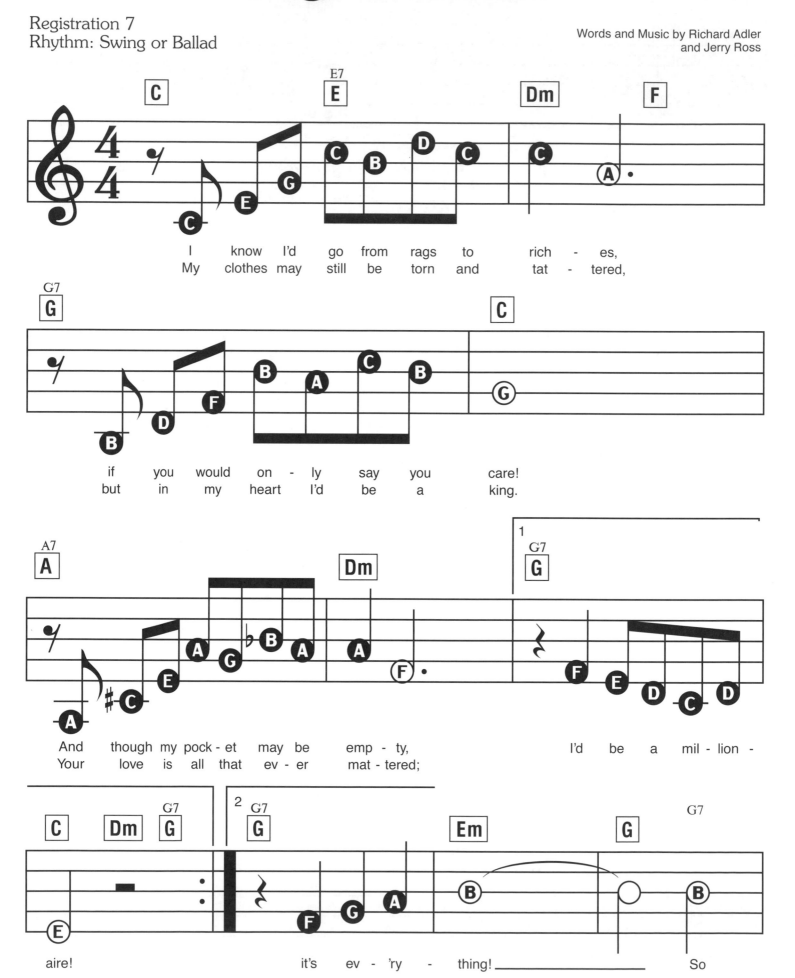

© Copyright 1953 (Renewed 1981) J & J Ross Company LLC and Lakshmi Puja Music Ltd.
All Rights Reserved   Used by Permission

39

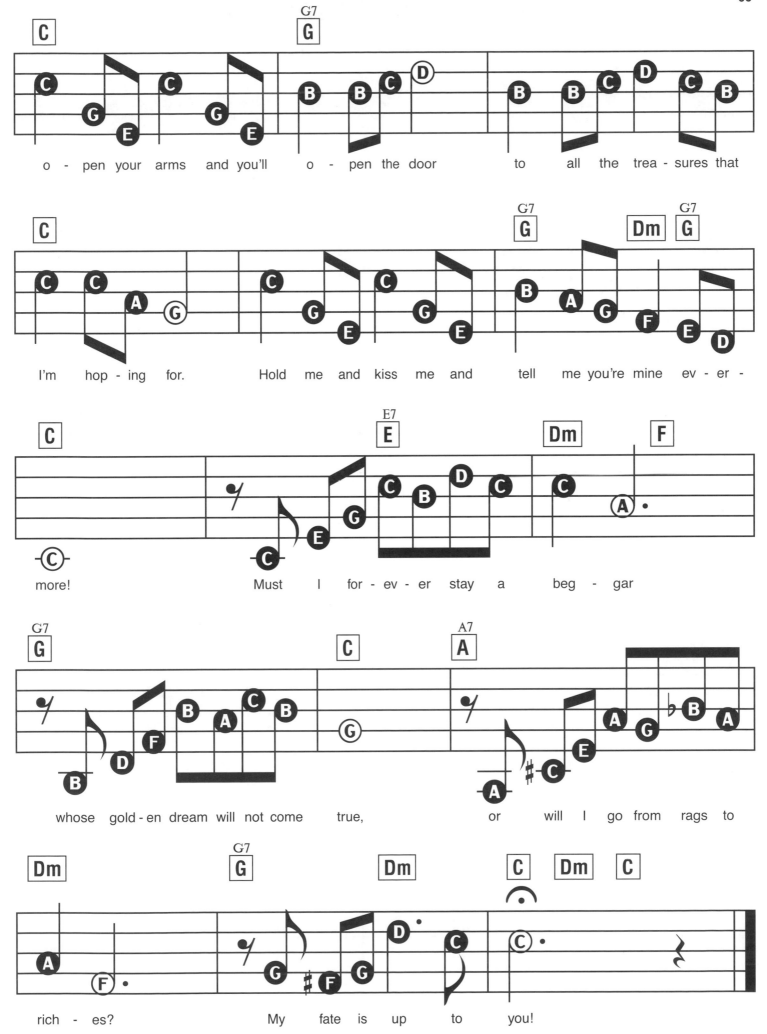

Sing, You Sinners
Theme from the Paramount Picture SING, YOU SINNERS

Registration 9
Rhythm: Fox Trot or Polka

Words and Music by Sam Coslow
and W. Franke Harling

Copyright © 1930 Sony/ATV Music Publishing LLC
Copyright Renewed
All Rights Administered by Sony/ATV Music Publishing LLC, 424 Church Street, Suite 1200, Nashville, TN 37219
International Copyright Secured   All Rights Reserved

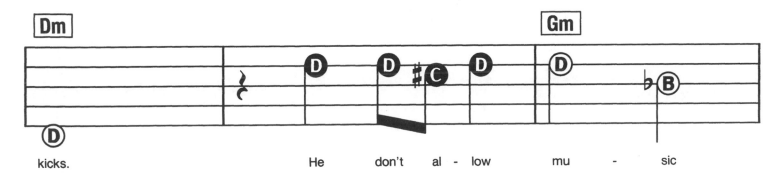

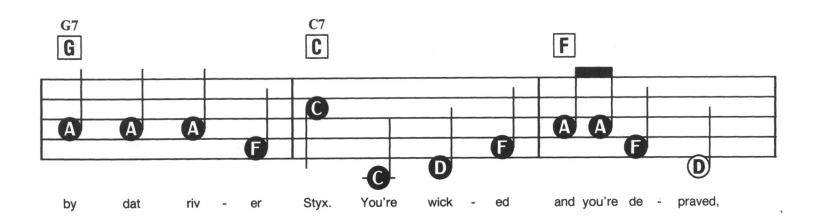

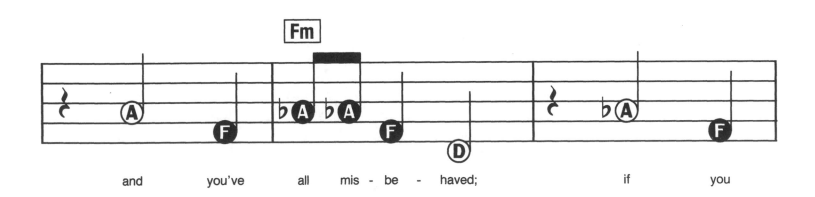

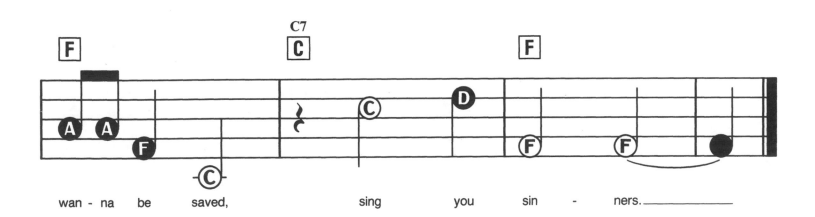

Smile

Registration 9
Rhythm: Ballad or Fox Trot

Words by John Turner and Geoffrey Parsons
Music by Charles Chaplin

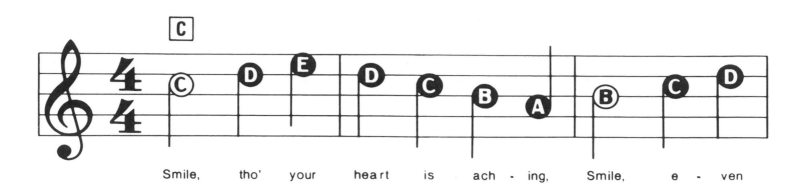

Smile, tho' your heart is ach - ing, Smile, e - ven

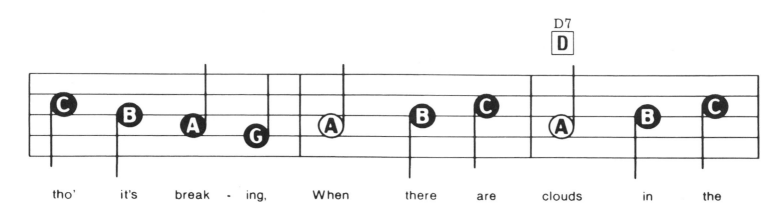

tho' it's break - ing, When there are clouds in the

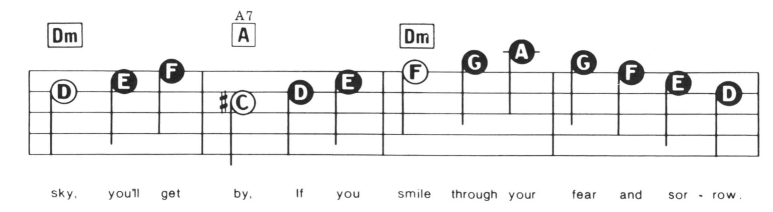

sky, you'll get by, If you smile through your fear and sor - row.

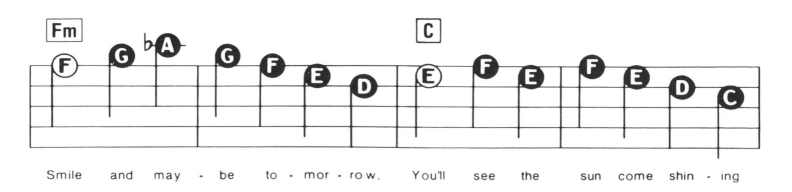

Smile and may - be to - mor - row, You'll see the sun come shin - ing

Copyright © 1954 by Bourne Co. (ASCAP)
Copyright Renewed
International Copyright Secured All Rights Reserved

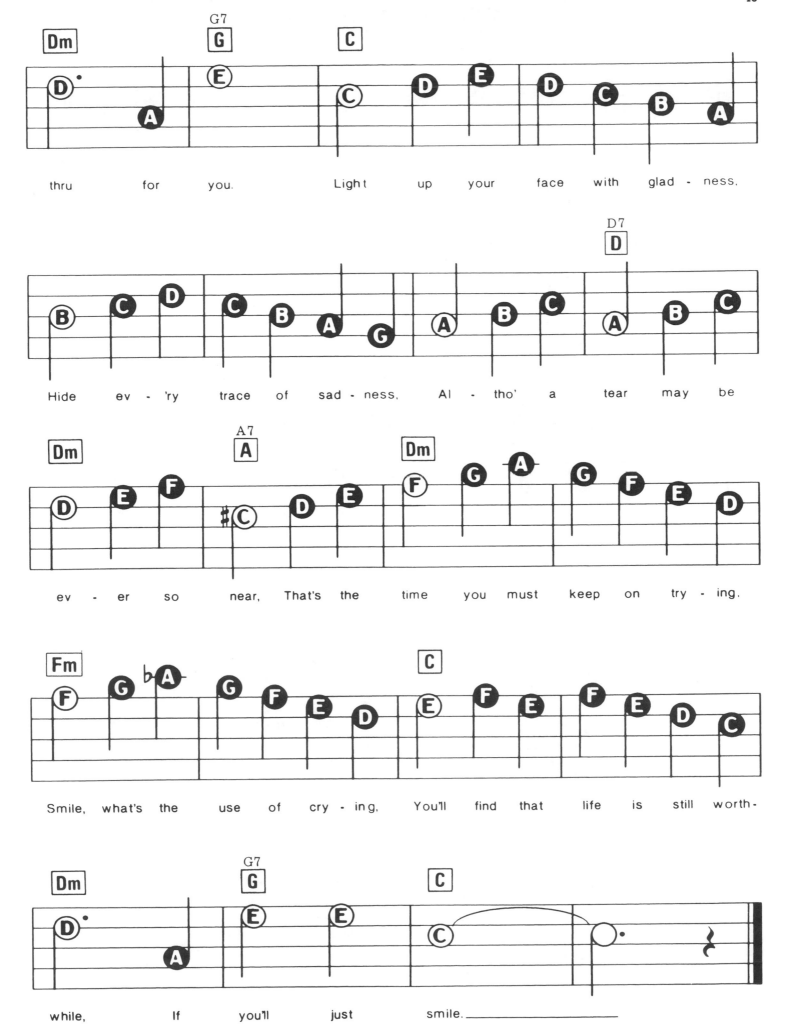

Something

Registration 4
Rhythm: Rock

Words and Music by
George Harrison

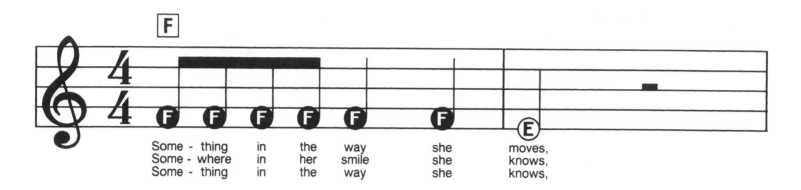

Some - thing in the way she moves,
Some - where in her smile she knows,
Some - thing in the way she knows,

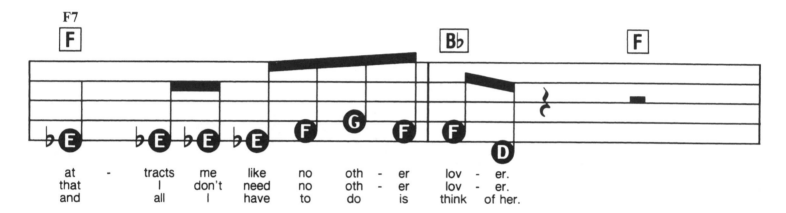

at - tracts me like no oth - er lov - er.
that I me don't like need no oth - er lov - er.
and all I have to do is think of her.

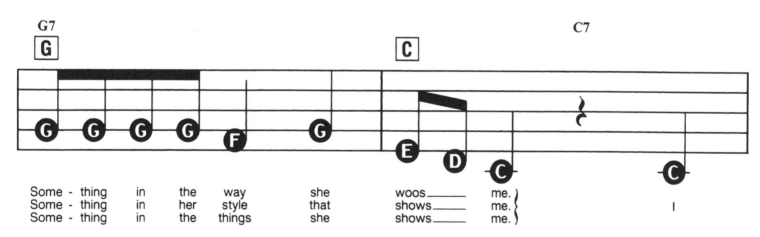

Some - thing in the way she woos___ me.
Some - thing in her way style that shows___ me.
Some - thing in the things she shows___ me.

I

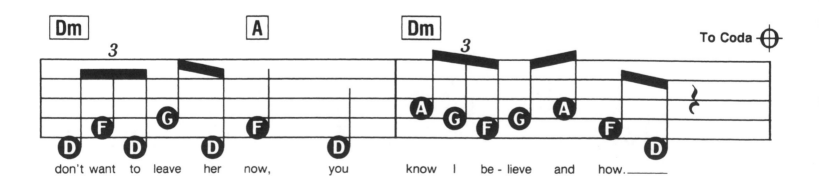

To Coda

don't want to leave her now, you know I be - lieve and how.___

Copyright © 1969 Harrisongs Ltd.
Copyright Renewed
All Rights Reserved

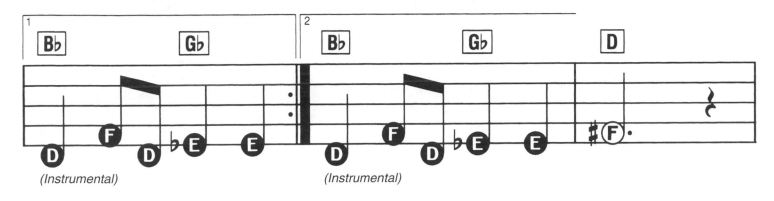

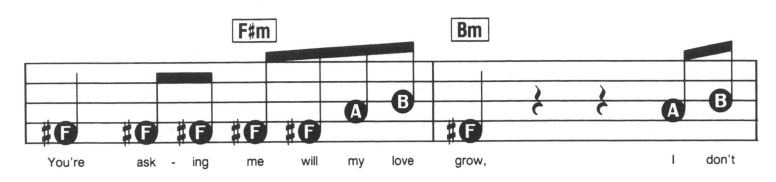

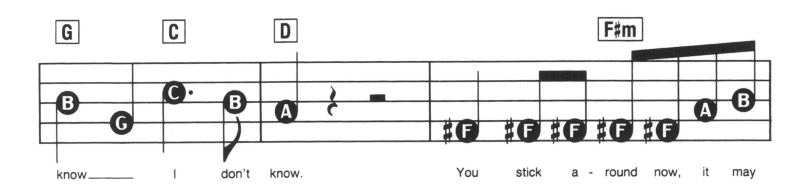

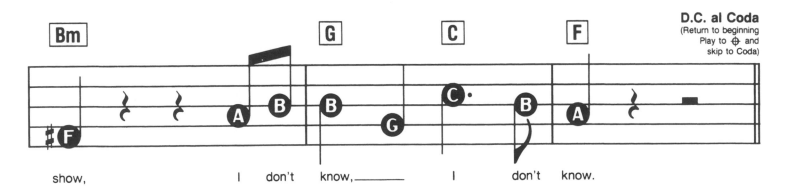

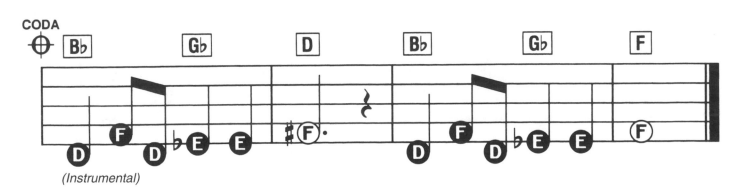

Steppin' Out with My Baby
from the Motion Picture Irving Berlin's EASTER PARADE

Registration 9
Rhythm: Swing

Words and Music by
Irving Berlin

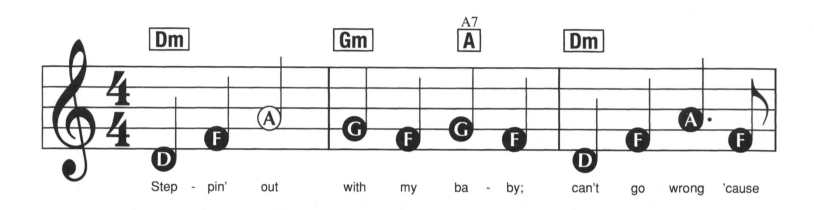

Step - pin' out with my ba - by; can't go wrong 'cause

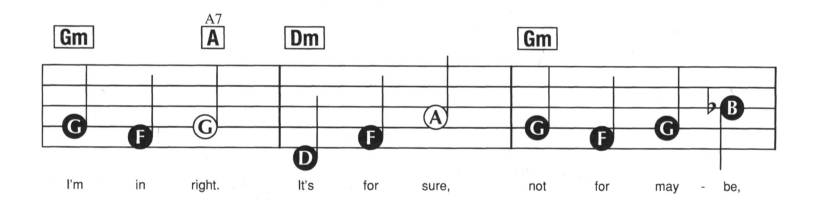

I'm in right. It's for sure, not for may - be,

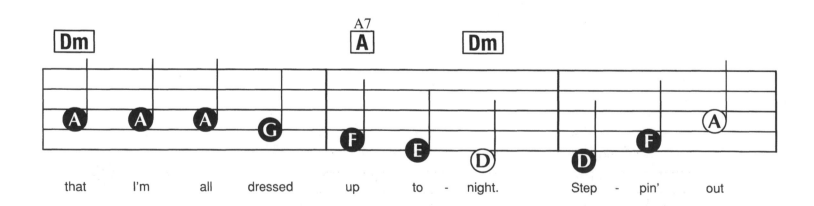

that I'm all dressed up to - night. Step - pin' out

© Copyright 1947 by Irving Berlin
Copyright Renewed
International Copyright Secured   All Rights Reserved

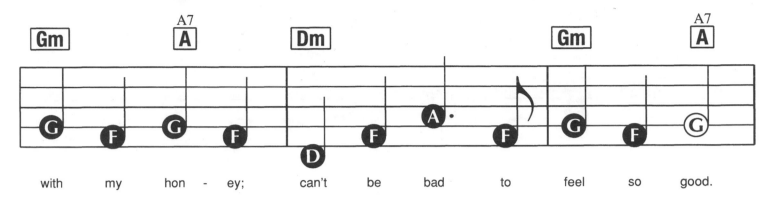

with my hon - ey; can't be bad to feel so good.

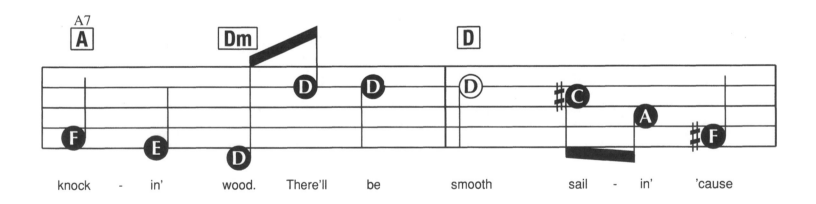

Nev - er felt quite so sun - ny, and I keep on

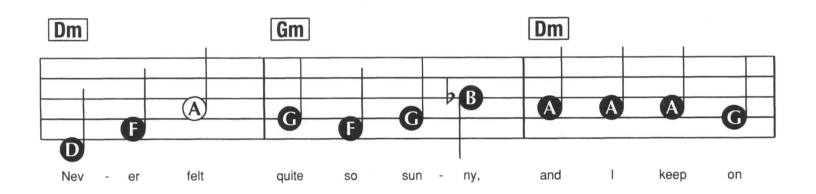

knock - in' wood. There'll be smooth sail - in' 'cause

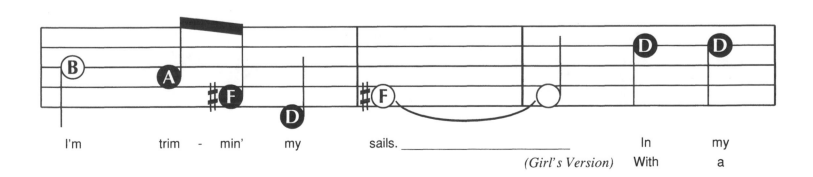

I'm trim - min' my sails. In my

(Girl's Version) With a

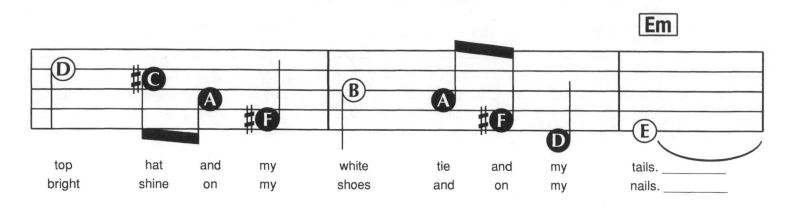

top hat and my white tie and my tails. _____
bright shine on my shoes and on my nails. _____

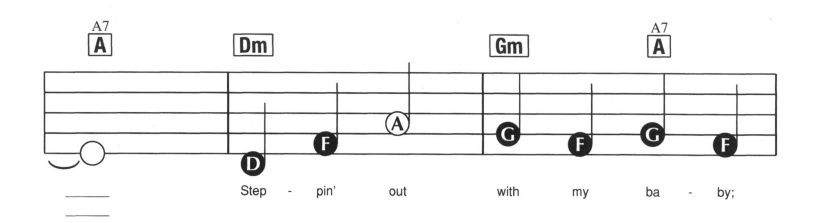

_____ Step - pin' out with my ba - by;

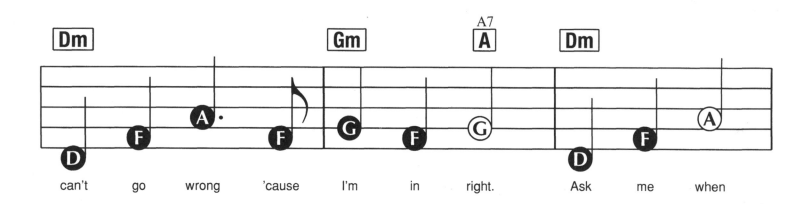

can't go wrong 'cause I'm in right. Ask me when

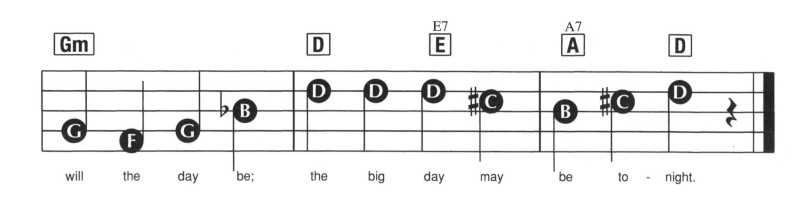

will the day be; the big day may be to - night.

Stranger in Paradise
from KISMET

Registration 10
Rhythm: 8-Beat, Pops or Ballad

Words and Music by Robert Wright and George Forrest
(Music Based on Themes of A. Borodin)

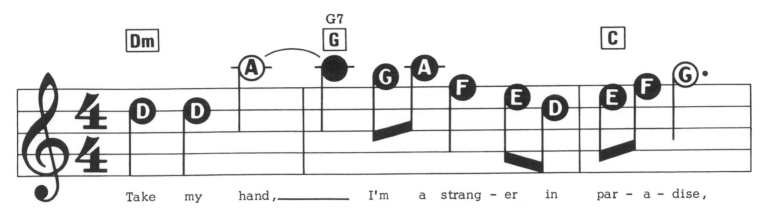

Take my hand, _____ I'm a strang - er in par - a - dise,

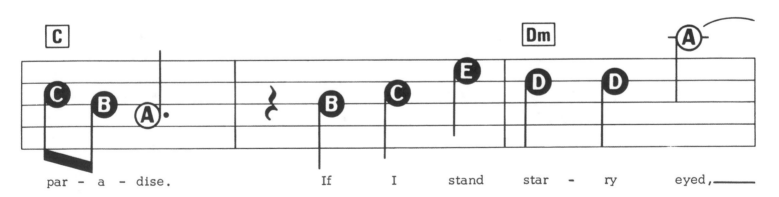

All lost in a won - der - land, _____ A strang - er in

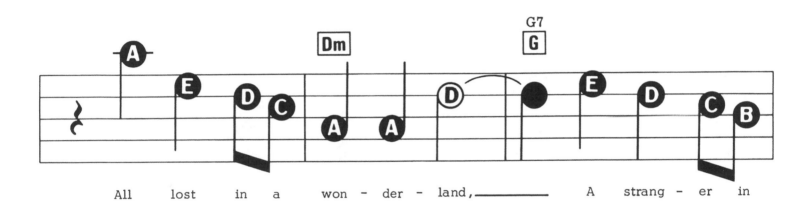

par - a - dise. If I stand star - ry eyed, _____

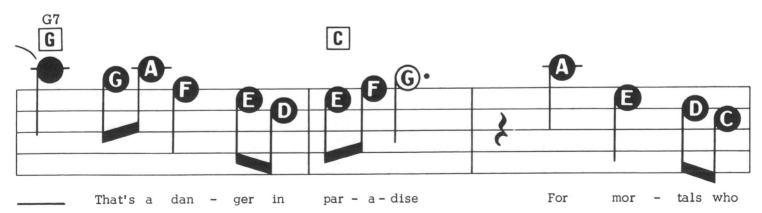

_____ That's a dan - ger in par - a - dise For mor - tals who

Copyright © 1953 Frank Music Corp.
Copyright Renewed and Assigned to Scheffel Music Corp., New York, NY
All Rights Controlled by Scheffel Music Corp.
All Rights Reserved Used by Permission

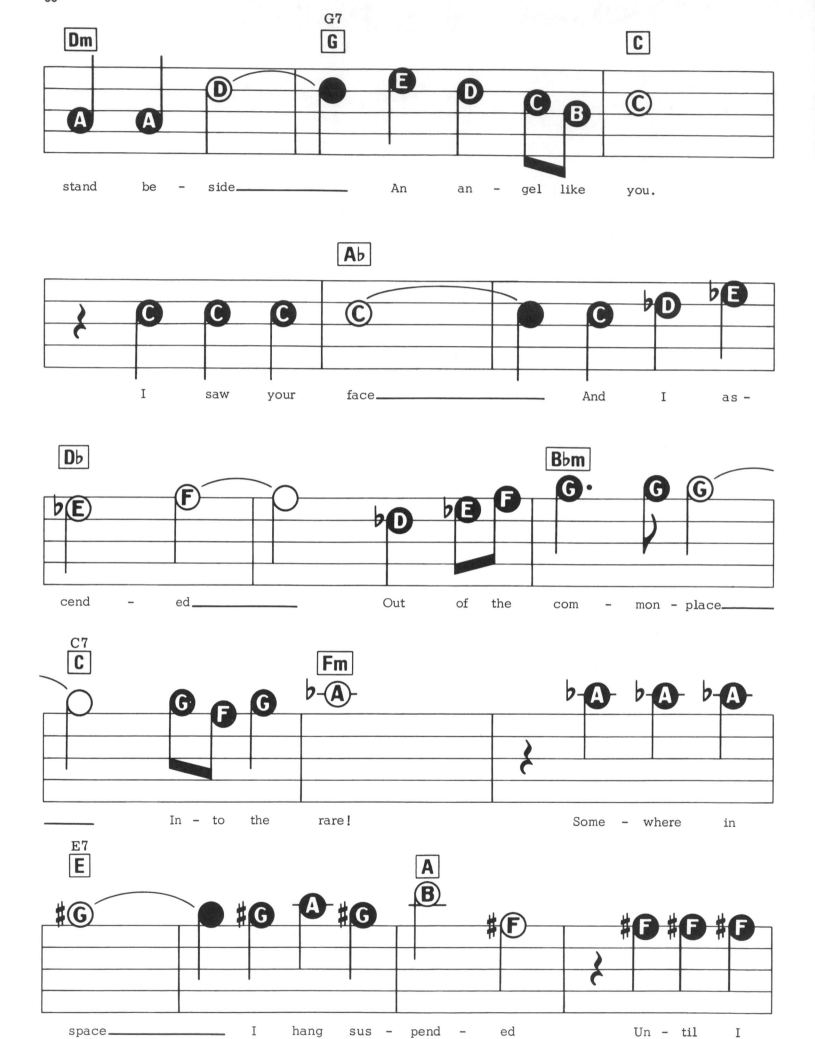

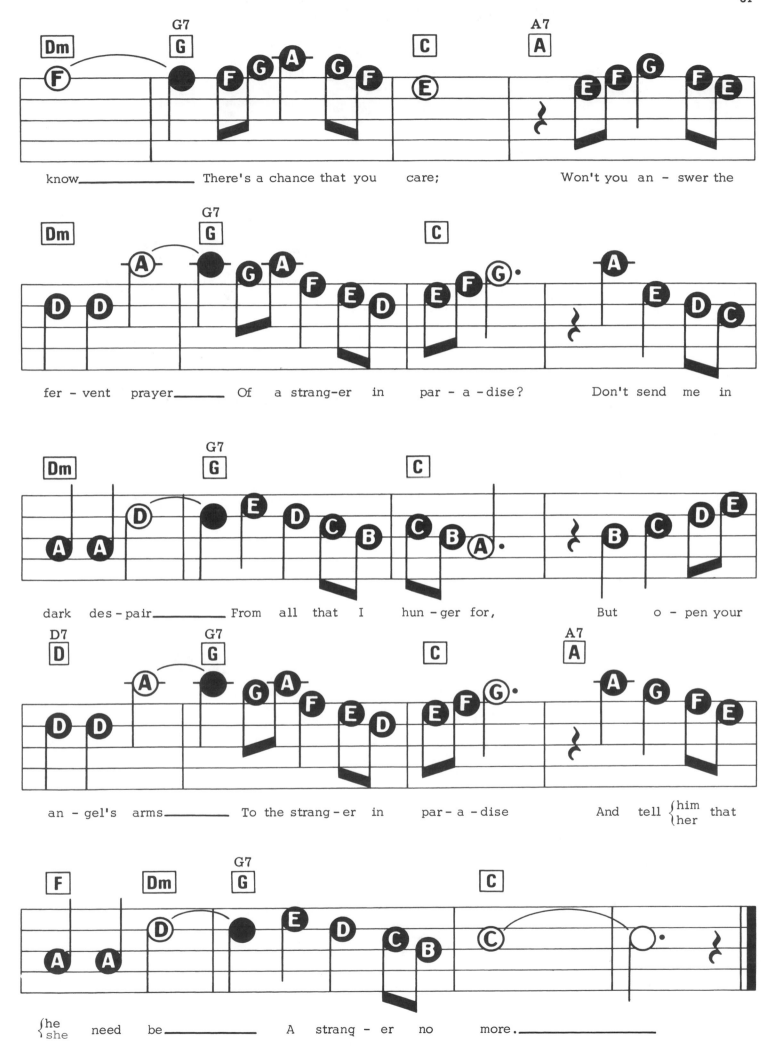

Where Do I Begin
(Love Theme)
from the Paramount Picture LOVE STORY

Registration 3
Rhythm: 4/4 Ballad or 8-Beat

Words by Carl Sigman
Music by Francis Lai

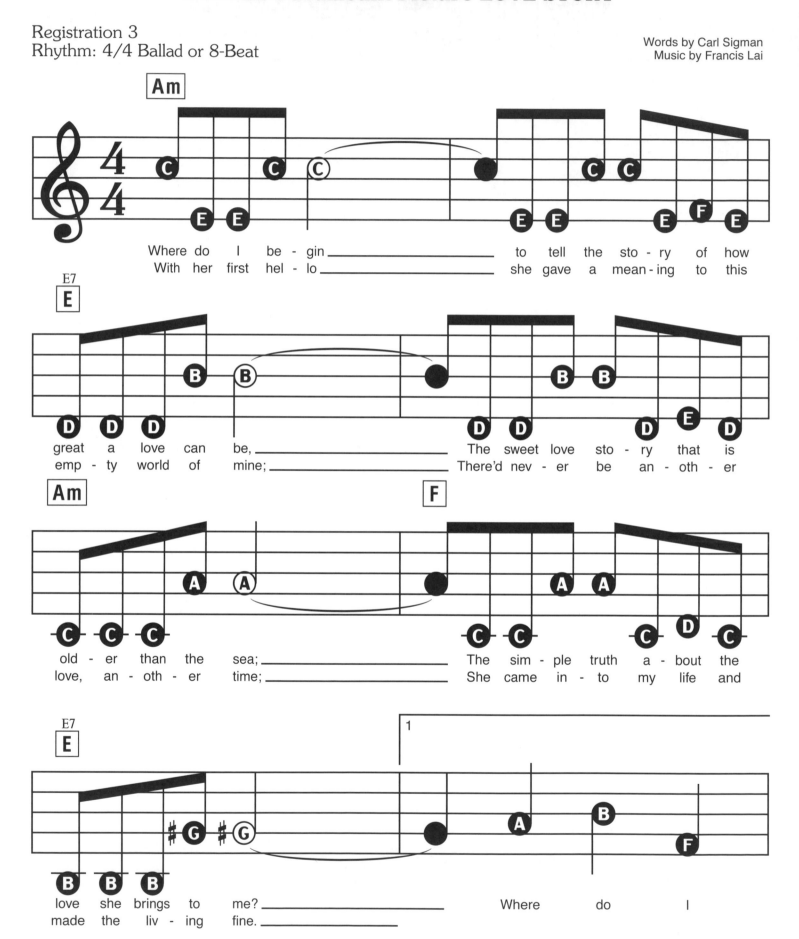

Copyright © 1970, 1971 Sony/ATV Music Publishing LLC
Copyright Renewed 1998, 1999 and Assigned to Sony/ATV Music Publishing LLC and Music Sales Corporation
All Rights on behalf of Sony/ATV Music Publishing LLC Administered by Sony/ATV Music Publishing LLC, 424 Church Street, Suite 1200, Nashville, TN 37219
International Copyright Secured   All Rights Reserved

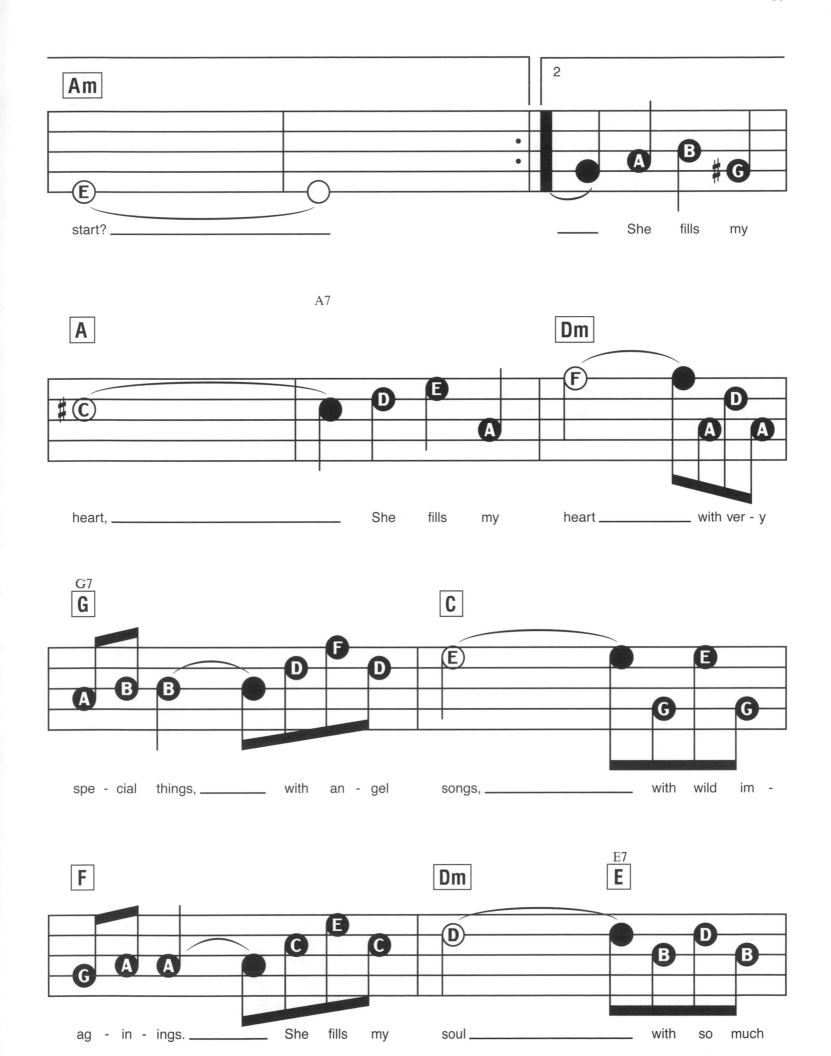

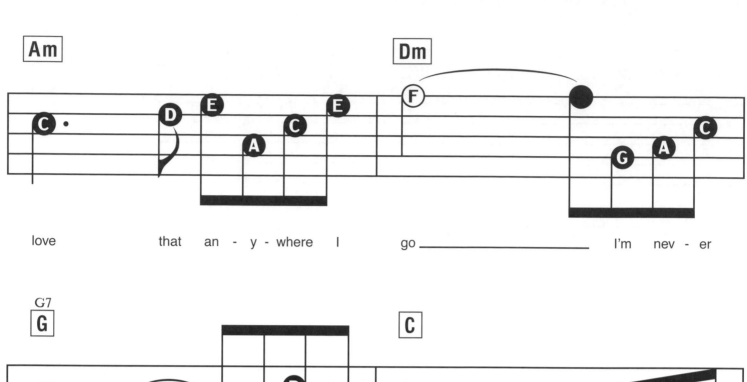

love   that   an - y - where   I   go _____ I'm nev - er

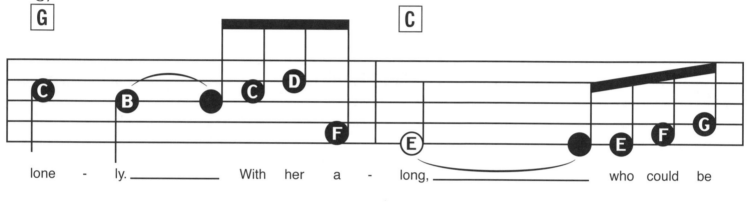

lone - ly. _____ With   her   a - long, _____ who   could   be

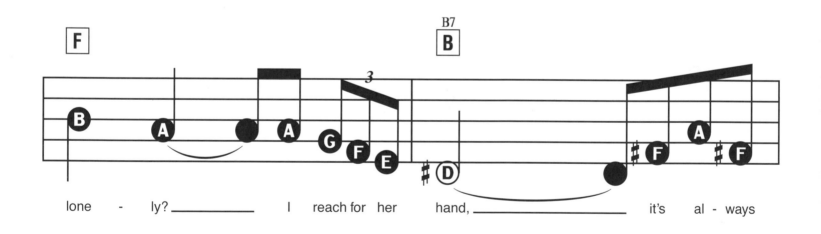

lone - ly? _____ I   reach for   her   hand, _____ it's   al - ways

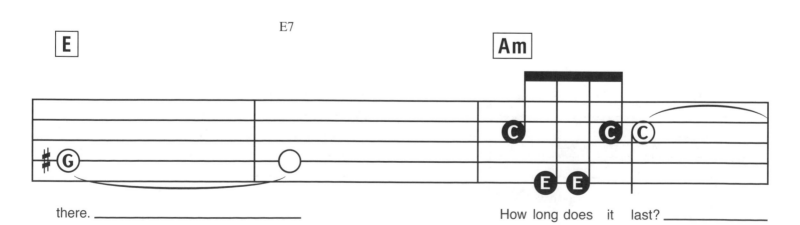

there. _____   How long does   it   last? _____

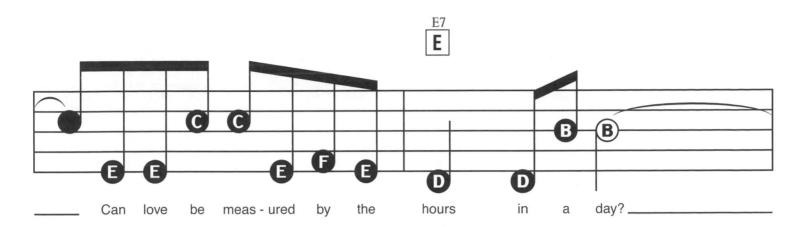

Can love be meas-ured by the hours in a day?

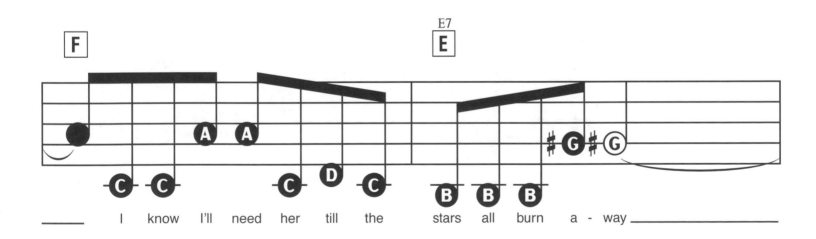

I have no an-swers now, but this much I can say:

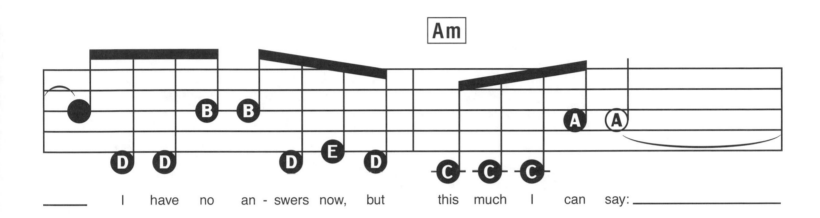

I know I'll need her till the stars all burn a-way

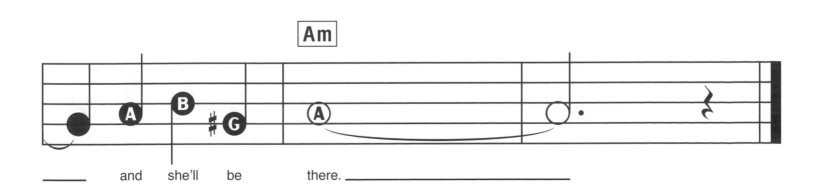

and she'll be there.

Who Can I Turn To
(When Nobody Needs Me)
from THE ROAR OF THE GREASEPAINT — THE SMELL OF THE CROWD

Registration 10
Rhythm: Ballad

Words and Music by Leslie Bricusse
and Anthony Newley

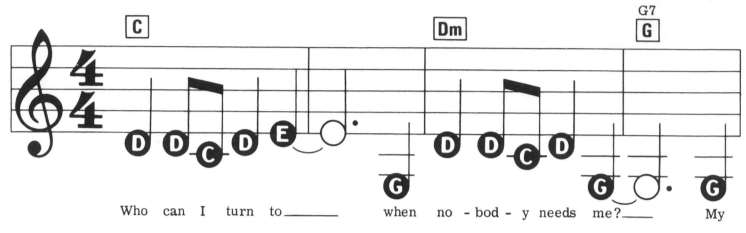

Who can I turn to _____ when no-bod-y needs me? _____ My

heart wants to know and so I must go where des-ti-ny leads me. _____

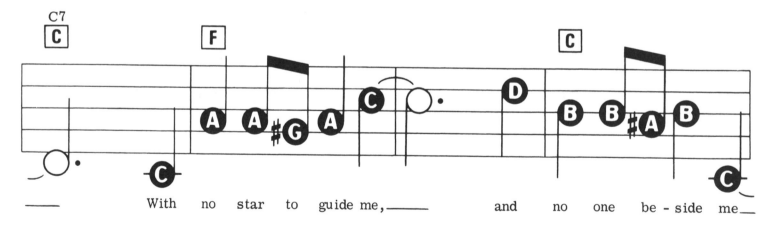

_____ With no star to guide me, _____ and no one be-side me

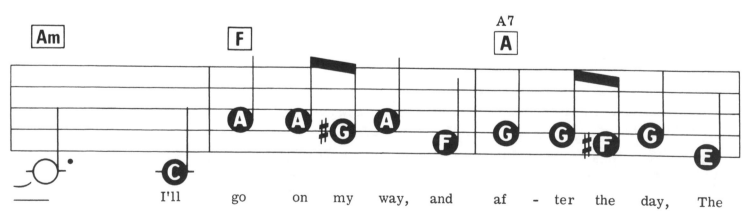

_____ I'll go on my way, and af-ter the day, The

© 1964 (Renewed) Concord Music Ltd., London, England
TRO - Musical Comedy Productions, Inc., New York, controls all publication rights for the U.S.A. and Canada
International Copyright Secured
All Rights Reserved Including Public Performance For Profit
Used by Permission

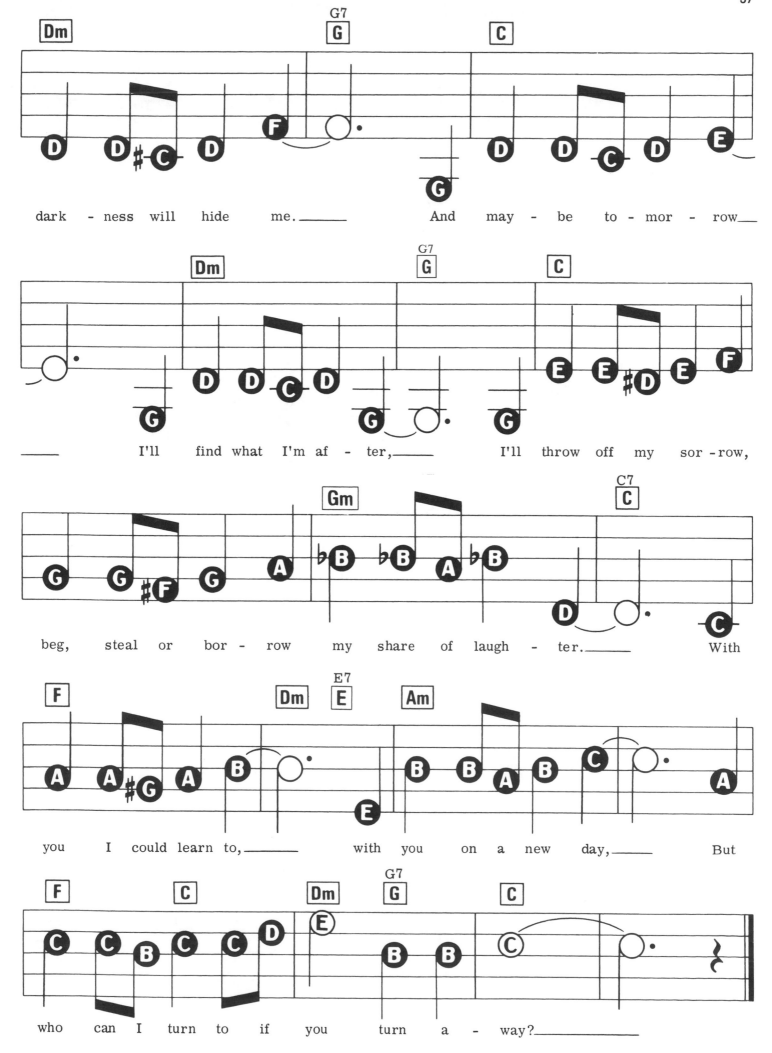

Take the "A" Train

Registration 4
Rhythm: Swing

Words and Music by
Billy Strayhorn

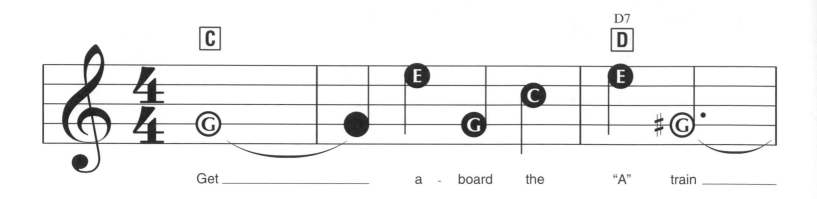

Get _____ a - board the "A" train _____

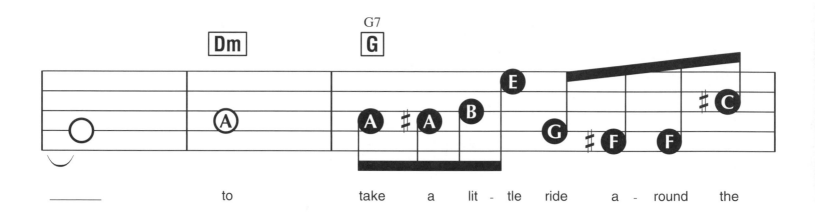

_____ to take a lit - tle ride a - round the

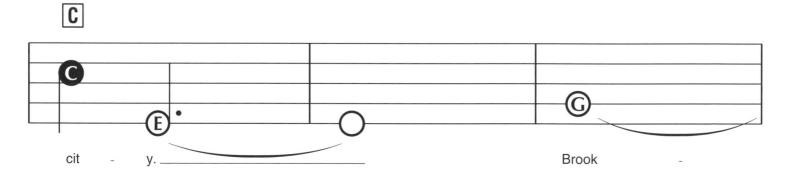

cit - y. _____ Brook -

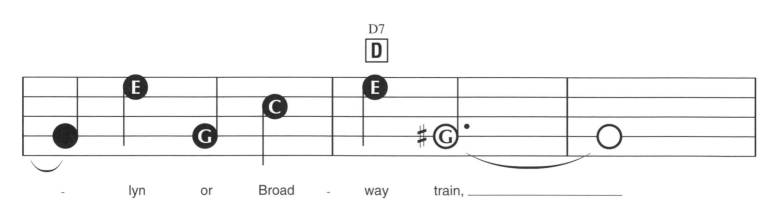

- lyn or Broad - way train, _____

Copyright © 1941 Reservoir Media Management, Inc. and Billy Strayhorn Songs, Inc.
Copyright Renewed
All Rights Administered by Reservoir Media Management, Inc.
All Rights Reserved   Used by Permission

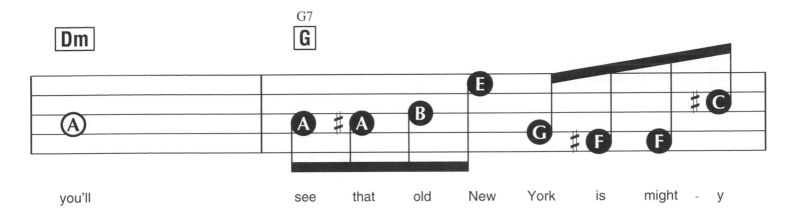

you'll see that old New York is might - y

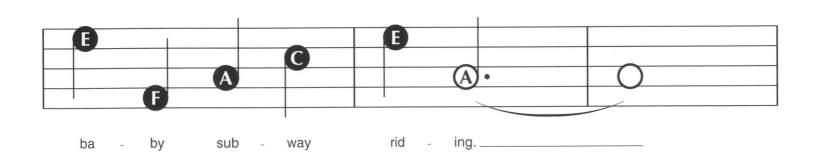

pret - ty. ____ Take your

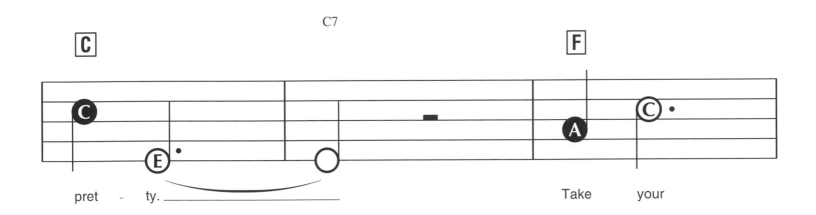

ba - by sub - way rid - ing. ____

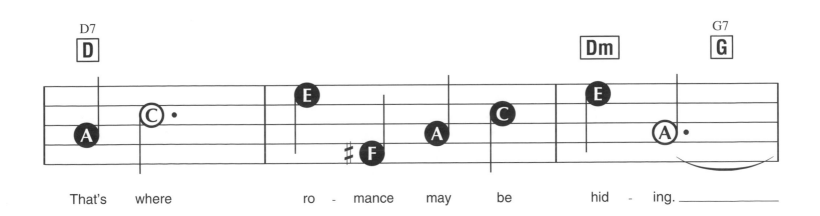

That's where ro - mance may be hid - ing. ____

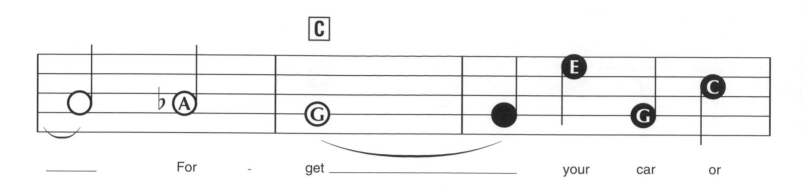

For - get _____ your car or

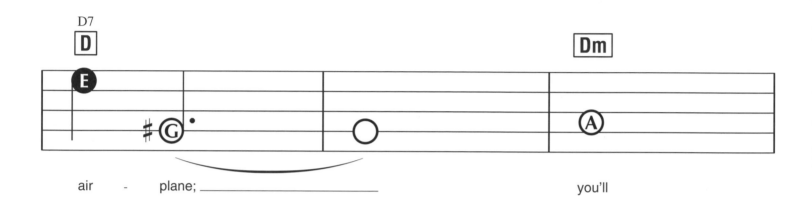

air - plane; _____ you'll

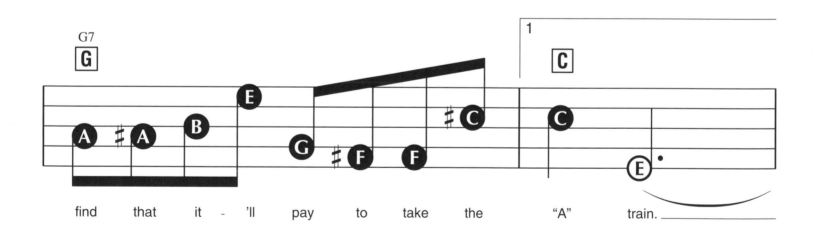

find that it - 'll pay to take the "A" train. _____

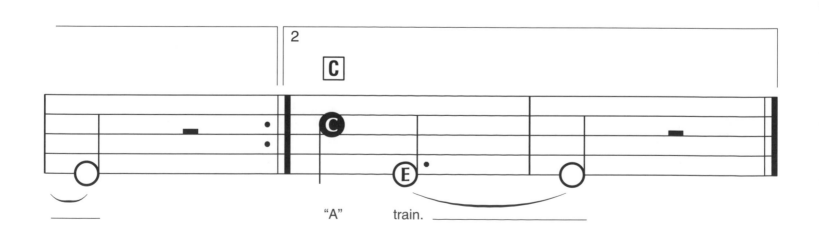

"A" train. _____

FOR ORGANS, PIANOS & ELECTRONIC KEYBOARDS

E-Z PLAY® TODAY PUBLICATIONS

The E-Z Play® Today songbook series is the shortest distance between beginning music and playing fun! Check out this list of highlights and visit www.halleonard.com for a complete listing of all volumes and songlists.

00102278	1. Favorite Songs with 3 Chords	$9.99
00100374	2. Country Sound	$12.99
00100382	4. Dance Band Greats	$7.95
00100305	5. All-Time Standards	$8.99
00282553	6. Songs of The Beatles – 3rd Edition	$14.99
00100442	7. Hits from Musicals	$8.99
00100490	8. Patriotic Songs	$8.99
00236235	9. Christmas Time – 2nd Edition	$9.99
00198012	10. Songs of Hawaii	$12.99
00137580	11. 75 Light Classical Songs	$19.99
00110284	12. Star Wars	$9.99
00100248	13. Three-Chord Country Songs	$14.99
00241118	15. Simple Songs	$14.99
00266435	16. Broadway's Best – 3rd Edition	$12.99
00100415	17. Fireside Singalong	$14.99
00149113	18. 30 Classical Masterworks	$8.99
00137780	19. Top Country Songs	$12.99
00102277	20. Hymns	$9.99
00197200	21. Good Ol' Gospel	$12.99
00100570	22. Sacred Sounds	$8.99
00234685	23. First 50 Songs You Should Play on Keyboard	$14.99
00249679	24. Songs with 3 Chords	$14.99
00140724	25. Happy Birthday to You and Other Great Songs	$10.99
14041364	26. Bob Dylan	$12.99
00001236	27. 60 of the World's Easiest to Play Songs with 3 Chords	$9.99
00101598	28. Fifty Classical Themes	$9.99
00100135	29. Love Songs	$9.99
00100030	30. Country Connection	$12.99
00160720	33. Ragtime Classics	$9.99
00100253	34. Inspirational Ballads	$10.95
00100122	36. Good Ol' Songs	$10.95
00100410	37. Favorite Latin Songs	$8.99
00156394	38. Best of Adele	$10.99
00159567	39. The Best Children's Songs Ever	$17.99
00119955	40. Coldplay	$10.99
00287762	41. Bohemian Rhapsody	$14.99
00100123	42. Baby Boomers Songbook	$10.99
00100576	43. Sing-along Requests	$9.99
00102135	44. Best of Willie Nelson	$12.99
00156236	46. 15 Chart Hits	$12.99
00100343	48. Gospel Songs of Johnny Cash	$7.95
00236314	49. Beauty and the Beast	$12.99
00102114	50. Best of Patsy Cline	$9.99
00100208	51. Essential Songs – The 1950s	$17.95
00100209	52. Essential Songs – The 1960s	$17.95
00199268	54. Acoustic Songs	$12.99
00100342	55. Johnny Cash	$12.99
00137703	56. Jersey Boys	$12.99
00100118	57. More of the Best Songs Ever	$17.99
00100285	58. Four-Chord Songs	$10.99
00100353	59. Christmas Songs	$10.99
00100304	60. Songs for All Occasions	$16.99
00100409	62. Favorite Hymns	$7.99
00278397	63. Classical Music – 2nd Edition	$7.99
00100223	64. Wicked	$12.99
00100217	65. Hymns with 3 Chords	$7.99
00232258	66. La La Land	$12.99
00100218	67. Music from the Motion Picture Ray	$8.95
00100449	69. It's Gospel	$9.99
00100432	70. Gospel Greats	$8.99
00236744	71. 21 Top Hits	$12.99
00100117	72. Canciones Románticas	$10.99
00147049	74. Over the Rainbow & 40 More Great Songs	$12.99
00100568	75. Sacred Moments	$6.95
00100572	76. The Sound of Music	$9.99
00238941	77. The Andrew Lloyd Webber Sheet Music Collection	$12.99
00248709	79. Roadhouse Country	$12.99
00265488	86. Leonard Cohen	$12.99

00100286	87. 50 Worship Standards	$14.99
00100287	88. Glee	$9.99
00100577	89. Songs for Children	$8.99
00290104	90. Elton John Anthology	$16.99
00100034	91. 30 Songs for a Better World	$10.99
00100288	92. Michael Bublé – Crazy Love	$10.99
00100219	95. The Phantom of the Opera (Movie)	$12.99
00100263	96. Mamma Mia – Movie Soundtrack	$9.99
00109768	98. Flower Power	$16.99
00275360	99. The Greatest Showman	$12.99
00119237	103. Two-Chord Songs	$9.99
00147057	104. Hallelujah & 40 More Great Songs	$12.99
00139940	106. 20 Top Hits	$12.99
00100256	107. The Best Praise & Worship Songs Ever	$16.99
00100363	108. Classical Themes (English/Spanish)	$7.99
00102232	109. Motown's Greatest Hits	$12.95
00101566	110. Neil Diamond Collection	$14.99
00100119	111. Season's Greetings	$15.99
00101498	112. Best of The Beatles	$19.99
00100134	113. Country Gospel USA	$12.99
00101612	115. The Greatest Waltzes	$9.99
00100136	118. 100 Kids' Songs	$14.99
00100433	120. Gospel of Bill & Gloria Gaither	$14.95
00100333	121. Boogies, Blues and Rags	$9.99
00100146	122. Songs for Praise & Worship	$8.95
00100001	125. Great Big Book of Children's Songs	$14.99
00101563	127. John Denver's Greatest Hits	$12.99
00116947	128. John Williams	$10.99
00140764	129. Campfire Songs	$12.99
00116956	130. Taylor Swift Hits	$10.99
00102318	131. Doo-Wop Songbook	$12.99
00100306	133. Carole King	$12.99
00288978	135. Mary Poppins Returns	$10.99
00291475	136. Disney Fun Songs	$14.99
00100144	137. Children's Movie Hits	$9.99
00100038	138. Nostalgia Collection	$14.95
00100289	139. Crooners	$19.99
00101946	143. The Songs of Paul McCartney	$8.99
00140768	144. Halloween	$10.99
00147061	147. Great Instrumentals	$9.99
00100152	151. Beach Boys – Greatest Hits	$12.99
00101592	152. Fiddler on the Roof	$9.99
00140981	153. Play Along with 50 Great Songs	$14.99
00101549	155. Best of Billy Joel	$12.99
00100315	160. The Grammy Awards Record of the Year 1958-2010	$19.99
00100293	161. Henry Mancini	$10.99
00100049	162. Lounge Music	$10.95
00100295	163. The Very Best of the Rat Pack	$12.99
00277916	164. The Best Christmas Songbook – 3rd Ed.	$9.99
00101895	165. Rodgers & Hammerstein Songbook	$10.99
00149300	166. The Best of Beethoven	$8.99
00149736	167. The Best of Bach	$8.99
00100148	169. A Charlie Brown Christmas™	$10.99
00101537	171. Best of Elton John	$9.99
00100321	173. Adele – 21	$12.99
00100149	176. Charlie Brown Collection™	$9.99
00102325	179. Love Songs of The Beatles	$12.99
00149881	180. The Best of Mozart	$8.99
00101610	181. Great American Country Songbook	$16.99
00001246	182. Amazing Grace	$12.99
00450133	183. West Side Story	$9.99
00100151	185. Carpenters	$12.99
00101606	186. 40 Pop & Rock Song Classics	$12.95
00100155	187. Ultimate Christmas	$18.99
00102276	189. Irish Favorites	$9.99
00100053	191. Jazz Love Songs	$9.99
00123123	193. Bruno Mars	$10.99
00124609	195. Opera Favorites	$8.99
00101609	196. Best of George Gershwin	$14.99
00119857	199. Jumbo Songbook	$24.99

00295070	200. Best Songs Ever – 8th Edition	$19.99
00101540	202. Best Country Songs Ever	$17.99
00101541	203. Best Broadway Songs Ever	$19.99
00101542	204. Best Easy Listening Songs Ever	$17.99
00100059	210. '60s Pop Rock Hits	$14.99
14041777	211. The Big Book of Nursery Rhymes & Children's Songs	$15.99
00126895	212. Frozen	$9.99
00101546	213. Disney Classics	$15.99
00101533	215. Best Christmas Songs Ever	$19.99
00131100	216. Frank Sinatra Centennial Songbook	$19.99
00100156	219. Christmas Songs with 3 Chords	$9.99
00102080	225. Lawrence Welk Songbook	$9.95
00101581	235. Elvis Presley Anthology	$16.99
00100158	243. Oldies! Oldies! Oldies!	$12.99
00100041	245. Best of Simon & Garfunkel	$9.99
00100296	248. The Love Songs of Elton John	$12.99
00102113	251. Phantom of the Opera (Broadway)	$14.95
00100203	256. Very Best of Lionel Richie	$10.99
00100302	258. Four-Chord Worship	$9.99
00100178	259. Norah Jones – Come Away with Me	$12.99
00100063	266. Latin Hits	$7.95
00100062	269. Love That Latin Beat	$8.99
00101425	272. ABBA Gold – Greatest Hits	$9.99
00102248	275. Classical Hits – Bach, Beethoven & Brahms	$7.95
00100186	277. Stevie Wonder – Greatest Hits	$10.99
00100237	280. Dolly Parton	$10.99
00100068	283. Best Jazz Standards Ever	$15.95
00281046	284. The Great American Songbook – The Singers	$19.99
00100244	287. Josh Groban	$14.99
00100022	288. Sing-a-Long Christmas	$12.99
00100023	289. Sing-a-Long Christmas Carols	$10.99
00102124	293. Movie Classics	$10.99
00100303	295. Best of Michael Bublé	$14.99
00100075	296. Best of Cole Porter	$9.99
00102130	298. Beautiful Love Songs	$9.99
00259570	301. Kid's Songfest – 2nd Edition	$12.99
00110416	302. More Kids' Songfest	$12.99
00102147	306. Irving Berlin Collection	$16.99
00100194	309. 3-Chord Rock 'n' Roll	$8.95
02501515	312. Barbra – Love Is the Answer	$10.99
00100197	315. VH1's 100 Greatest Songs of Rock & Roll	$19.95
00100277	325. Taylor Swift	$10.99
00100092	333. Great Gospel Favorites	$8.99
00100278	338. The Best Hymns Ever	$19.99
00100280	341. Anthology of Rock Songs	$19.99
00102235	346. Big Book of Christmas Songs	$14.95
00100095	359. 100 Years of Song	$19.99
00100096	360. More 100 Years of Song	$19.95
00159568	362. Songs of the 1920s	$19.99
00159569	363. Songs of the 1930s	$19.99
00159570	364. Songs of the 1940s	$19.99
00159571	365. Songs of the 1950s	$19.99
00159572	366. Songs of the 1960s	$19.99
00159573	367. Songs of the 1970s	$19.99
00159574	368. Songs of the 1980s	$19.99
00159575	369. Songs of the 1990s	$19.99
00159576	370. Songs of the 2000s	$19.99
00159577	371. Songs of the 2010s	$19.99
00100103	375. Songs of Bacharach & David	$8.99
00100107	392. Disney Favorites	$19.99
00100108	393. Italian Favorites	$9.99
00100111	394. Best Gospel Songs Ever	$19.99
00100115	400. Classical Masterpieces	$10.99

HAL•LEONARD®

Prices, contents, and availability subject to change without notice.

0519

330